The Joy of Cherries

by Theresa Millang

Adventure Publications, Inc.
Cambridge, Minnesota

With Special Appreciation.

I have included my own cherry recipes in this collection as well as those from across the country. Thank you for sharing your favorite recipes.

Book and Cover Design by Jonathan Norberg

10 9 8 7 6 5 4 3 2 1
Copyright 2006 by Theresa Nell Millang
Published by Adventure Publications, Inc.
820 Cleveland Street South
Cambridge, Minnesota 55008
1-800-678-7006
www.adventurepublications.net

ISBN-13: 978-1-59193-145-4
ISBN-10: 1-59193-145-2
Printed in China

Table of Contents

OTHER DESSERTS

MEALS PAIRED WITH CHERRIES

PIES, PASTRIES

Pies

Pastries

GELATIN SALADS, OTHER SALADS, SOUPS

Gelatin Salads

Other Salads

Introduction

Cherry trees in full flower are one of the beautiful signs of spring. The fruits, which are excellent in both sweet and savory recipes, are ready for harvest in just a few months. Aside from being delicious, cherries have also been discovered to contain compounds that can ease the pain of arthritis, regulate circadian rhythm, fight cancer and more. Enjoy tasty and nutritious cherries!

Cherry History and Facts

A Bit of Cherry History

Although there are native cherry species in North America (they're typically called pin or bird cherries), the ancestors of commercially grown cherry trees likely originated in Europe and western Asia. Cherries were a popular food with Chinese nobility. These trees reached Greece through trade and were cultivated there by about 300 BC. Romans, who are also credited with introducing apple trees across their vast empire, helped speed the spread of cherry trees.

Descendants of early cherry trees reached the New World with Spanish missionaries. These missionaries are responsible for some of California's earliest cherry groves. Settlers brought the next wave of cherry pits and saplings from their homeland. Along with apples and other fruits, cherries gradually spread west.

Cherry Production

Two types of cherries are grown commercially: sweet cherries and tart cherries (also called pie or sour cherries). There are over a thousand sweet cherry varieties, and some of the best-known include Bing, Van, Lambert, Rainier and Royal Ann. Montmorency is the most popular variety of sour cherry; others are Balaton, Northstar and Meteor. Both types of cherries reach peak ripeness in late July. Currently, the U.S. produces more than 650 million pounds of cherries a year.

California, Oregon and Washington are the leaders in sweet cherry production, while the Great Lakes states of Michigan, Wisconsin, New York and Pennsylvania dominate tart cherry production. Other states that commercially produce cherries are Idaho, Montana and Utah. Michigan produces nearly three-quarters of the nation's tart cherries. A Presbyterian minister named Peter Dougherty planted the first groves in 1852 near Traverse City (now called the

Cherry Capital of the World). To the surprise of many, the groves flourished. Lake Michigan tempered the climate, keeping the groves from getting too hot or too cold. Commercial tart cherry groves and a processing facility soon followed.

Door County, in eastern Wisconsin, had a sizeable tart cherry industry by the 1860s. By the late 1950s, Door County had 10,000 acres of groves. Though there are fewer groves now, Wisconsin remains the fourth-largest tart cherry producer in the U.S. To this day, nearly all of Wisconsin's cherries are grown in Door County.

What are Maraschino Cherries?

Maraschino cherries are candied fresh cherries. They originated in Yugoslavia and northern Italy and became a great delicacy in fine American establishments. The original style of maraschino cherries were packed in liqueur. Yankee ingenuity kicked in, along with Prohibition, and by the 1920s the American style of maraschino cherry, which was packed in sugar syrup and flavored with almond, was the nation's favorite.

Washington, D.C.'s Famous Cherry Trees

Cherry blossom time, usually during late March and early April, is highly celebrated in Washington, D.C. These famous cherry trees had their roots in a diplomatic expression of friendship between the U.S. and Japan. Ms. Eliza Scidmore, who had spent considerable time in Japan and was fond of the beautiful cherry trees there, originally suggested that cherries be planted along the Potomac. When her suggestion failed to have any effect, she decided to raise the money to buy imported cherry trees from Dr. David Fairchild. Dr. Fairchild had been testing the hardiness of two types of Japanese cherries, and was an enthusiastic supporter.

Ms. Scidmore wrote of her plans to First Lady Helen Taft, who took up the idea and was soon promised that she would have the trees. Famous Japanese chemist Jokichi Takamine was visiting D.C. with consul Mr. Midzuno. When they learned that Japanese cherries would be planted in the city, they offered to ship 2,000 cherry trees. Unfortunately, this first shipment of trees was infected and had to be burned. But in 1912, more than 3,000 trees were shipped and soon planted. The famous Cherry Blossom Festival began in 1935. Nearly 4,000 additional cherry trees were given as a gift to Lady Bird Johnson in 1965.

Cherry Fun Facts

A cherry tree takes 10–15 years to reach full fruit-bearing capacity.

An average cherry tree produces close to 7,000 cherries, enough for 28 pies.

It takes about 250 cherries to make one pie.

Cherries are part of the Rose family, in the Prunus genus. They are most closely related to plums, peaches, apricots and almonds.

February is National Cherry Month.

The National Cherry Festival is held in July in Traverse City, Michigan, and lasts for a week.

Tart cherry trees are self-pollinating. Sweet cherry trees require cross-pollination, not only between male and female trees, but also among different varieties.

The Health Benefits of Cherries

Like so many fruits and vegetables, cherries are an excellent source of antioxidants. Antioxidants stabilize free radicals. While we produce free radicals by our own biological processes, excessive free radicals can build up in our bodies. An overabundance of free radicals can speed up the natural aging process and lead to a host of health troubles.

But recent research has shown that the Montmorency tart cherry, in particular, contains several compounds that other fruits don't. While research continues, the early discoveries hint at exciting possibilities:

Handle the pain of arthritis and gout: Cherries contain anthocyanins, a class of compounds that gives them their rich color. The particular anthocyanins in tart cherries have shown that they effectively block the same inflammation- and pain-causing enzymes that traditional pain killers such as aspirin and ibuprofen target. Many arthritis and gout sufferers find relief from their joint pain and side effects of drugs by utilizing tart cherries.

Regulate circadian rhythms: Tart cherries contain relatively high amounts of melatonin, a chemical compound that we produce in the pineal gland at the base of our brains. Melatonin regulates wakefulness during the day and restfulness at night; it gives our bodies a pattern. As we age, our bodies produce less melatonin. If we have a melatonin imbalance we may suffer from insufficient rest. The melatonin in tart cherries is a way to supplement the body's production and help maintain a natural circadian rhythm.

Stunt the growth of cancer: Perillyl alcohol (POH), found in tart cherries, appears to help the body remove cancer-causing substances before tumors develop. In addition, perillyl alcohol has also demonstrated an ability to slow and reduce cancer cell growth by depriving these abnormal cells of the proteins they use to reproduce. POH has shown this ability with every type of cancer it was tested against.

The anthocyanins in tart cherries have also shown promise in reducing the risk for type-2 diabetes, heart attacks and stroke.

Cherry Tips

Buying
Buy cherries that are plump, glossy and firm. If possible, buy cherries that still have green stems. Avoid cherries with blemishes; they will spoil faster.

Storing
For fresh eating, store unwashed cherries in the refrigerator for as long as a week (though they're most flavorful if used within a few days). Wash cherries right before you eat them.

You can freeze cherries whole, either pitted or unpitted, depending on how you want to use them later. Wash the cherries, remove stems and pits (if desired). Place on a baking sheet so that they do not touch each other. Freeze and place in heavy plastic food bags or freezer containers. Frozen cherries will be good for about ten months.

Cherries can also be frozen with a sugar-pack method. Wash, stem and pit the cherries. Sprinkle each quart with about ¾ cup granulated sugar, pack into containers and freeze.

To dry cherries, wash them, cut them in half and remove the stem and pit. Place skin-side down in single layers on dehydrator trays. Dry the cherry halves at 140° for 6–12 hours, being careful to not over-dry them. They should be leathery and slightly sticky. Seal in small plastic food bags and keep in a cool, dry place.

How to Pit Cherries

If you're using fresh cherries for a recipe that requires pitted fruit, there are a number of methods you can try:

Cut the cherry in half and pry out the pit

Scoop out the pit using the tip of a vegetable peeler

Use a wire loop tool homemade out of an old-fashioned hairpin
(some people swear by this method!)

Use a cherry pitter specifically designed for the job, available at many cooking and food supply stores

Cherry Equivalents

1 pound fresh unpitted cherries = about 80 cherries
1 pound fresh unpitted cherries = 2⅓ cups pitted
1 pound fresh unpitted cherries = 1½ cups cherry juice
16 ounces canned cherries = 1½ cups
21 ounces canned cherry pie filling = 1½ cups
10 ounces frozen cherries = 1 cup
2 ounces dried cherries = ½ cup

Planting

Native cherries grow in most places in the U.S., but cultivated cherries require specific conditions to produce a fruit crop. It is best to consult with a local extension service, university horticultural department or plant nursery to see if cultivated cherries will do well in your area. Cultivated cherry trees thrive mostly in the northern tier of the U.S. They do not tolerate extreme cold, but require a dormant winter period. They prefer moist, well-drained soil and relatively dry air.

Sources: American Chemical Society's Journal of Agriculture and Food Chemistry, In the News Press Release, "Chemicals Found in Cherries May Help Fight Diabetes." http://pubs.acs.org/pressrelease/jafc/release3.html (Accessed 04/27/06); Cherry Marketing Institute's Cherry Advantage Newsletters, www.cherrymkt.org/health/ (Accessed 04/27/06); Door County Chamber of Commerce, "Door County Cherries Fact Sheet." www.doorcountyvacations.com/html/generalInfo/sportsAndNature/cherryInfo.htm (Accessed 04/27/06); The Fruit Institute, www.fruitinstitute.org/cherries.htm (Accessed 04/27/06); National Park Service, "History of the Cherry Trees in Washington, D.C." www.nps.gov/nacc/cherry/history.htm (Accessed 04/27/06); Orchard of Health's Cherry Library, www.orchardofhealth.com/cherry.htm (Accessed 04/27/06)

Appetizers

BRIE TORTE

Perfect for that special party.

1 16-ounce round Brie

⅓ cup chopped dried tart cherries
¼ cup finely chopped toasted pecans
½ teaspoon dried thyme
6 tablespoons butter, softened

Chill Brie until firm. Cut in half horizontally.

Mix remaining ingredients in a small bowl until well blended. Spread mixture evenly on cut side of one piece of Brie. Top with remaining Brie, cut side down. Press together. Wrap in food plastic wrap, and refrigerate 1 hour before serving. Cut into wedges. Serve at room temperature. Refrigerate leftovers.

Makes 20 servings.

CHERRY CHICKEN PIZZA

Serve this appetizer hot.

1½ cups thinly sliced leeks
2 tablespoons butter

1 12-inch pre-baked pizza crust
1 tablespoon olive oil

½ cup dried tart cherries
1½ cups skinless, boneless chicken breast, cooked and chopped
¾ cup walnuts, toasted
1 cup grated mozzarella cheese
¾ cup grated smoked gouda cheese

Preheat oven to 450°.

Stir and cook leeks in butter until wilted.

Place crust in a pizza baking pan. Brush olive oil evenly over crust. Top evenly with wilted leeks. Sprinkle with cherries, chicken and walnuts. Top with mozzarella cheese, then with gouda cheese. Bake until cheese is melted, about 7 minutes. Refrigerate leftovers.

Makes 12 servings.

CHICKEN CHERRY WRAPS

Serve as an appetizer or with a crisp salad for a light lunch.

½ cup nonfat lemon yogurt
1 tablespoon honey mustard
1 teaspoon Worcestershire sauce
¾ teaspoon curry powder
¼ teaspoon salt
¼ teaspoon coarsely ground black pepper

1½ cups finely chopped fully cooked chicken
1 cup dried tart cherries
½ cup finely chopped seeded cucumber
⅓ cup shredded carrot
¼ cup sliced green onions

4 8-inch tomato flavored flour tortillas

Mix first six ingredients in a bowl until blended. Stir in remaining ingredients except tortillas. Spoon ¾ cup mixture onto each tortilla. Fold in sides. Roll up jellyroll style.

Makes 4 servings.

CITRUS DIP WITH FRESH CHERRIES

A fresh appetizer.

1 cup dairy sour cream
2 tablespoons granulated sugar
1 tablespoon fresh lime juice
2 teaspoons freshly grated lime peel

fresh sweet cherries, strawberries, and grapes

Stir sour cream, sugar, lime juice and lime peel in a small bowl. Cover and refrigerate until chilled. Serve with fresh cherries, strawberries and grapes. Refrigerate leftovers.

Makes 4 servings.

FRESH CHERRY CANAPES

Pretty simple...and delicious.

1 3-ounce package cream cheese, softened
2 tablespoons finely chopped walnuts
1 tablespoon fresh orange juice
½ teaspoon freshly grated orange peel

16 slices party rye bread
4 slices thinly sliced ham, cut into 4 triangles
16 pitted fresh sweet cherries

Mix cream cheese, walnuts, orange juice and orange peel in a bowl.

Spread about ½ tablespoon mixture on each slice of bread. Place one piece of ham on top of cheese mixture. Top each with a pitted cherry; secure with a toothpick. Refrigerate leftovers.

Makes 16 servings.

SENSATIONAL STUFFED MUSHROOMS

Serve these elegant mushrooms hot from the oven.

28 large mushrooms

½ pound bulk pork sausage
1 cup chopped dried tart cherries
2 green onions, thinly sliced
1 8-ounce package cream cheese, softened

Preheat oven to 425°.
Rinse mushrooms. Pat dry. Remove stem from mushrooms.

Cook and stir sausage in a large saucepan over medium heat until sausage is well done. Remove from heat; drain fat. Add cherries, green onions and cream cheese; mix well. Fill each mushroom with a heaping teaspoonful of mixture. Place on a lightly greased baking sheet. Bake for 6–8 minutes. Refrigerate leftovers.

Makes 28 appetizers.

Bars
Cookies

CANDIED CHERRIES CHEESECAKE BARS

Perfect for the holidays.

1 cup all-purpose flour
⅓ cup brown sugar, packed
⅓ cup butter, softened

1 8-ounce package cream cheese, softened
¼ cup granulated sugar
1 egg
1 tablespoon fresh lemon juice
½ teaspoon pure vanilla extract
¼ cup chopped green candied cherries
¼ cup chopped red candied cherries

Preheat oven to 350°.
Beat flour, brown sugar and butter in a small bowl with an electric mixer on low speed until well mixed. Reserve ½ cup crumb mixture; set aside. Press remaining crumb mixture onto bottom of an ungreased 8x8-inch baking pan. Bake 10–12 minutes or until lightly browned. Remove from oven.

Beat cream cheese, granulated sugar, egg, lemon juice and vanilla in a medium bowl with an electric mixer on medium speed until smooth. Stir in cherries by hand. Spread mixture over partially baked crust. Sprinkle with reserved crumb mixture. Return to oven; bake 18–20 minutes or until filling is set. Remove from oven; cut into bars while warm. Store covered in the refrigerator.

Makes 25 bars.

CHAMPION CHERRY BARS

Tart cherries and pecans...good bar.

1 cup margarine
¾ cup granulated sugar
¾ cup brown sugar, packed
2 eggs
1 teaspoon pure vanilla extract

2¼ cups all-purpose flour
1 teaspoon baking powder
⅛ teaspoon salt
1 12-ounce package vanilla milk chips
2 cups dried tart cherries
1 cup coarsely chopped pecans

Preheat oven to 350°.
Grease a 15x10x1-inch baking pan.

Beat margarine and sugars in a large bowl with an electric mixer on medium speed until well blended. Beat in eggs and vanilla extract.

Mix flour, baking powder and salt in a medium bowl; gradually beat mixture into creamy mixture on low speed. Stir in vanilla chips, cherries and pecans by hand. Spread dough evenly into prepared pan. Bake 20 minutes or until light golden. Do not over bake. Remove from oven. Cool in pan. Cut into bars. Refrigerate leftovers.

Makes 48 bars.

CHERRY ALMOND TOFFEE BARS

Sliced almonds and toffee in this cherry bar.

1½ cups all-purpose flour
½ cup powdered sugar
¾ cup cold butter

1 14-ounce can sweetened condensed milk
1 egg, beaten
1 teaspoon pure vanilla extract
1 cup sliced almonds
1 6-ounce package toffee chips
¾ cup dried tart cherries

Preheat oven to 350°.
Mix flour and powdered sugar in a medium bowl until blended. Cut in butter with a pastry blender until crumbly. Press mixture firmly onto bottom of an ungreased 13x9-inch baking pan. Bake 15 minutes. Remove from oven.

Mix sweetened condensed milk, egg and vanilla in a large bowl until blended. Stir in almonds, toffee chips and cherries. Spoon mixture over partially baked crust; spread evenly. Bake about 25 minutes or until golden. Remove from oven. Cool in pan on a wire rack. Cut into bars. Store in the refrigerator.

Makes 24 bars.

CHERRY CHOCOLATE CHIP COCONUT BARS

Maraschino cherries, chocolate and coconut in this good bar.

1½ cups graham cracker crumbs
½ cup butter or margarine, melted

1 14-ounce can sweetened condensed milk
1 cup semisweet chocolate chips
1 10-ounce jar maraschino cherries without stems,
   well drained and chopped
1⅓ cups flaked coconut

Preheat oven to 350°.
Mix graham cracker crumbs and butter in a small bowl; press mixture firmly onto bottom of an ungreased 13x9-inch baking pan.

Pour sweetened condensed milk evenly over crumb mixture in pan. Sprinkle evenly with chocolate chips. Sprinkle evenly with chopped cherries. Sprinkle evenly with coconut. Press down firmly with a fork. Bake 25 minutes or until lightly browned. Remove from oven. Cool in pan. Cut into bars. Refrigerate leftovers.

Makes 36 bars.

CHERRY CREAM BARS

Serve plain or top with thawed whipped topping when serving.

1 18.25-ounce package butter yellow cake mix
½ cup butter, softened
1 egg
¼ cup chopped pecans

1 8-ounce package cream cheese, softened
¼ cup powdered sugar
½ teaspoon pure vanilla extract
1 egg
1 16-ounce can cherry pie filling

Preheat oven to 350°.
Beat dry cake mix, butter and 1 egg in a large bowl with an electric mixer on low speed until crumbly. Stir in pecans. Press mixture into an ungreased 13x9-inch baking pan. Bake until set, about 6 minutes. Remove from oven.

Beat cream cheese, powdered sugar, vanilla and 1 egg in a medium bowl with an electric mixer on medium speed until smooth. Pour over crust in pan. Spoon cherry pie filling evenly over top. Bake 30–40 minutes or until golden light brown and filling is set. Remove from oven. Cool in pan. Cut into bars. Store in refrigerator.

Makes 36 bars.

CHERRY NUT BARS

Pecans and marshmallows in these cherry bars.

2 cups all-purpose flour
2 cups uncooked quick-cooking oats
1½ cups granulated sugar
1¼ cups butter, melted
½ cup chopped pecans
1 teaspoon baking soda

1 21-ounce can cherry pie filling
1 teaspoon pure vanilla extract
1 cup miniature marshmallows

Preheat oven to 350°.
Beat first six ingredients in a large bowl with an electric mixer on low speed until mixture forms coarse crumbs. Reserve 1½ cups crumb mixture; set aside. Press remaining crumb mixture into an ungreased 13x9-inch baking pan. Bake 12–15 minutes or until lightly browned on edges. Remove from oven.

Gently spoon pie filling over hot crust. Drizzle evenly with vanilla. Sprinkle evenly with marshmallows, then sprinkle with reserved crumb mixture. Return to oven and bake 25–35 minutes or until lightly brown. Remove from oven. Cool in pan. Cut into bars. Refrigerate leftovers.

Makes 36 bars.

CHOCOLATE CHERRY BARS

Chocolate and cherries...made for each other.

1 18.25-ounce package moist devils food cake mix
1 21-ounce can cherry pie filling
1 teaspoon pure vanilla extract or almond extract
3 eggs, beaten

Frosting
1 cup granulated sugar
⅓ cup whole milk
5 tablespoons butter
1 cup semisweet chocolate chips (6-ounces)
½ teaspoon pure vanilla extract

Preheat oven to 350°.
Grease and flour a 13x9-inch baking pan.

Mix dry cake mix, pie filling, 1 teaspoon vanilla and eggs in a large bowl until well blended. Pour mixture into prepared pan. Bake 25–35 minutes or until a wooden pick inserted in center comes out clean. Remove from oven.

Frosting: Mix sugar, milk and butter in a small saucepan. Bring mixture to a boil. Boil 1 minute stirring constantly. Remove from heat. Stir in chocolate chips until smooth. Stir in ½ teaspoon vanilla extract. Pour warm frosting over warm bars. Cool completely in pan. Cut into bars. Refrigerate leftovers.

Makes 36 bars.

FRUIT CAKE BARS

Red and green candied cherries in this fruit cake bar.

1 cup all-purpose flour
¾ cup brown sugar, packed
½ cup butter
1 teaspoon freshly grated
    orange peel
½ teaspoon baking soda
½ teaspoon ground cinnamon
¼ teaspoon salt
1 egg
1 teaspoon pure vanilla extract

¼ cup all-purpose flour
1½ cups red candied cherries
1 cup green candied cherries
1 8-ounce package pitted dates, cut up
½ cup golden raisins
1 cup coarsely chopped pecans

Glaze
⅓ cup butter
2 cups powdered sugar
1 teaspoon pure vanilla extract
½ teaspoon freshly grated orange peel
3–4 tablespoons hot orange juice,
    approximately

Preheat oven to 350°.
Grease and flour a 13x9-inch baking pan.

Mix first 9 ingredients in a large bowl until combined.

Mix ¼ cup flour, cherries, dates, raisins and pecans in another bowl; stir into large bowl mixture. Spread batter into prepared pan. Bake until a wooden pick inserted in center comes out clean, about 35 minutes. Remove from oven. Cool completely in pan on a wire rack.

Glaze: Heat butter in a saucepan until melted. Stir in sugar, vanilla, orange peel and about 3 tablespoons orange juice; beat to a drizzling consistency. Drizzle over cooled bars. Refrigerate leftovers.

Makes 24 bars.

MALTED CHOCOLATE CHIP CHERRY BARS

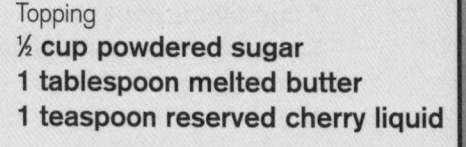

Malted milk powder and mini chocolate chips in this cherry bar.

¾ cup butter, softened
1 13-ounce jar chocolate malted
  milk powder
3 large eggs, beaten
1 teaspoon pure vanilla extract
¼ teaspoon almond extract

Topping
½ cup powdered sugar
1 tablespoon melted butter
1 teaspoon reserved cherry liquid

1¾ cups all-purpose flour
2 cups semisweet mini chocolate chips
2 6-ounce jars maraschino cherries without stems, drained and
  reserving liquid, then coarsely chop cherries

Preheat oven to 350°.
Grease a 13x9-inch baking pan.

In a large mixer bowl, beat butter with an electric mixer on medium speed 1 minute.
Gradually beat in malted milk powder until crumbly. Beat in eggs, 3 tablespoons
reserved cherry liquid, vanilla and almond extract.

Beat in flour until just combined. Fold in chocolate chips and chopped cherries by
hand. Pour batter into prepared pan; spread evenly. Bake 30–35 minutes or until
center is set. Remove from oven. Cool completely in pan on a wire rack. Drizzle
top with topping mixture. Cut into bars.

Topping: Mix topping ingredients in a small bowl. Stir, adding additional cherry liquid
as necessary to make a drizzling consistency.

Makes 24 bars.

TRIPLE CHOCOLATE CHERRY BARS

Frosted chocolate cherry bars...yum.

1 18.25-ounce package moist chocolate fudge cake mix
2 eggs, beaten
½ teaspoon pure vanilla extract
1 21-ounce can cherry pie filling
1 cup miniature semisweet chocolate chips

Frosting
3 cups powdered sugar
⅓ cup butter, softened
2 teaspoons pure vanilla extract
3 ounces melted and cooled unsweetened baking chocolate
4 tablespoons milk

Preheat oven to 350°.
Grease and flour a 15x10x1-inch jelly roll baking pan.

Mix dry cake mix, eggs, ½ teaspoon vanilla, pie filling and chocolate chips in a large bowl with a spoon until blended. Pour mixture into prepared pan; spread evenly. Bake 28–35 minutes or until a wooden pick inserted in center comes out clean. Remove from oven. Cool completely in pan. Spread with frosting. Cut into bars. Refrigerate leftovers.

Frosting: Beat frosting ingredients together in a bowl with an electric mixer until smooth.

Makes 48 bars.

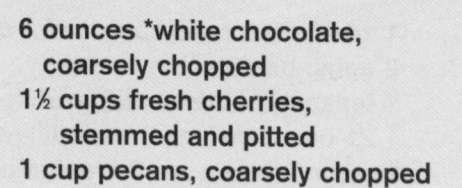

WHITE CHOCOLATE CHERRY PECAN BARS

For a special treat, serve with a scoop of butter pecan ice cream.

½ cup butter, softened
1 cup brown sugar, packed
2 eggs
⅔ cup dairy sour cream
1½ teaspoons pure vanilla extract

6 ounces *white chocolate,
  coarsely chopped
1½ cups fresh cherries,
  stemmed and pitted
1 cup pecans, coarsely chopped

1¼ cups all-purpose flour
1 teaspoon baking powder
½ teaspoon baking soda
½ teaspoon salt

2 ounces *white chocolate,
  coarsely chopped

Preheat oven to 350°.
Grease a 13x9-inch baking pan.

Beat butter and brown sugar in a bowl until creamy. Beat in eggs, one at a time.
Mix in sour cream and vanilla.

Mix flour, baking powder, baking soda and salt in a small bowl; gradually stir into
butter mixture. Stir in 6 ounces chocolate, cherries and pecans.

Pour batter into prepared pan. Bake 20 minutes or until golden. Cool completely.

Melt 2 ounces chocolate; drizzle over bars. Cut. Refrigerate leftovers.

Makes 24 bars.

*Select chocolate with cocoa butter for best flavor.

WHOLESOME GRANOLA BARS

A tasty wholesome snack.

1½ cups low fat granola
1 cup uncooked quick-cooking oats
¾ cup dried tart cherries
½ cup all-purpose flour
⅓ cup slivered almonds, toasted
½ teaspoon ground cinnamon

2 egg whites, slightly beaten
⅓ cup honey
¼ cup brown sugar, packed
2 tablespoons corn oil

Preheat oven to 350°.
Line bottom and sides of an 8x8-inch baking pan with cooking foil. Lightly spray with nonstick cooking spray.

Mix granola, oats, cherries, flour, almonds and cinnamon in a bowl until well blended.

In another bowl, stir egg whites, honey, brown sugar and corn oil until blended; add to mixture in large bowl and stir until all is coated. Press mixture evenly into prepared pan. Bake 20–25 minutes or until light brown. Remove from oven; cool in pan on a wire rack. Lift foil to remove bars from pan. Cool completely; cut into bars.

Makes 20 bars.

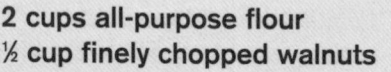

CHERRY BISCOTTI

These crunchy cookies are twice baked.

¾ cup granulated sugar
2 eggs
¼ cup corn oil
1 tablespoon fresh orange juice
2 teaspoons freshly grated
  orange peel
1½ teaspoons pure vanilla
  extract

2 cups all-purpose flour
½ cup finely chopped walnuts
1 teaspoon baking powder
¼ teaspoon salt
1 cup chopped dried tart cherries

1 egg white, beaten with 1 tablespoon
  cold water in a small bowl

Preheat oven to 350°.
Beat sugar and eggs in a large mixing bowl with an electric mixer on medium speed until thick and pale yellow, about 3 minutes. Add corn oil, orange juice, orange peel and vanilla; beat until blended.

Mix flour, walnuts, baking powder and salt; gradually beat into egg mixture on low speed until mixed. Stir in cherries by hand.

Place soft dough on a lightly floured surface; sprinkle lightly with additional flour. Shape into two 8x2-inch logs. Place logs 3–4 inches apart on a greased baking sheet; flatten tops slightly. Brush egg mixture on top. Sprinkle lightly with additional sugar. Bake 25–30 minutes, until light brown and firm to touch. Remove from oven. Cool on baking sheet 15 minutes.

Reduce heat to 300°.
Cut logs diagonally into ½-inch slices with a serrated knife. Place slices cut-side down on baking sheet. Bake 8–10 minutes; turn slices; bake 8–10 minutes or until golden. Remove from baking sheet; cool completely on a wire rack.

Makes about 2 dozen.

CHERRY CHEWBILEES

Offer these special cookies...to special people.

½ cup butter, softened
½ cup margarine, softened
¾ cup granulated sugar
¾ cup brown sugar, packed
2 eggs
1 teaspoon pure vanilla extract

2¼ cups all-purpose flour
1 teaspoon baking soda
⅛ teaspoon salt

1¾ cups coarsely chopped white chocolate (the kind with cocoa butter listed in ingredients)
1½ cups dried tart cherries
1 cup cashews, coarsely chopped

Preheat oven to 350°.

Beat butter, margarine, granulated sugar, brown sugar, eggs and vanilla in a large bowl with an electric mixer on medium speed until combined.

Mix flour, baking soda and salt in a medium bowl; gradually beat into first mixture on low speed until blended.

Stir in chocolate, cherries and cashews by hand. Drop by rounded tablespoonfuls onto ungreased baking sheets. Bake 10–12 minutes or until lightly browned. Do not over bake. Remove from baking sheets to a wire rack; cool completely.

Makes about 4 dozen

CHERRY COCONUT COOKIES

Almost candy...great for that holiday tray.

1 7-ounce package flaked coconut
2 tablespoons cornstarch
½ cup sweetened condensed milk
1 teaspoon pure vanilla extract
½ cup chopped red candied cherries

Preheat oven to 325°.
Grease and flour a baking sheet.

Mix coconut and cornstarch in a medium bowl. Stir in sweetened condensed milk and vanilla until combined. Stir in cherries.

Drop by small round teaspoonfuls 1 inch apart on prepared baking sheet. Bake 12–15 minutes or until lightly browned on bottoms. Remove from oven; cool on baking sheet 1 minute. Remove from baking sheet; cool completely on a wire rack.

Makes 2 dozen.

CHERRY-DATE SKILLET COOKIES

Skillet cookies...let the kids help.

1 cup butter
1 cup brown sugar, packed
1 8-ounce package chopped dates
1 egg

4 cups sweetened flaked coconut, divided
3 cups crisp rice cereal
½ cup chopped maraschino cherries, drained
1 tablespoon pure vanilla extract

Melt butter in a 12-inch skillet over medium heat. Stir in sugar and dates. Remove from heat. Stir in egg. Return to heat, and cook, stirring constantly until mixture come to a full boil, about 5 minutes. Boil, stirring constantly, 1 minute.

Remove from heat. Stir in 1 cup coconut, rice cereal, cherries and vanilla until moistened. Let stand 10 minutes. Shape rounded teaspoonfuls of mixture into 1-inch balls, then roll in remaining coconut placed in a bowl.

Makes 5 dozen.

CHEWY CHERRY-TOPPED COCONUT COOKIES

A nice cookie for that holiday tray...freeze them if making ahead of time.

1 cup butter, softened
¾ cup granulated sugar
¾ cup brown sugar, packed
2 eggs
1½ teaspoons pure vanilla extract

2¼ cups all-purpose flour
2 teaspoons baking powder
¼ teaspoon baking soda
2½ cups sweetened flaked coconut
30 red candied cherries, halved

Preheat oven to 350°.

Beat butter, sugars, eggs and vanilla in a large bowl on medium speed until creamy.

Add flour, baking powder and baking soda to bowl; beat on low speed until well blended. Stir in coconut by hand. Drop dough by rounded teaspoonfuls 2 inches apart onto ungreased baking sheets. Press 1 cherry half on top of each cookie. Bake 9–14 minutes or until edges are lightly browned. Remove from baking sheets to a wire rack.

Makes 5 dozen.

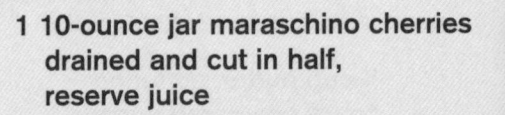

HIDDEN CHERRY COOKIES

A cherry half is tucked under chocolate frosting in this cookie.

¾ cup butter, softened
¾ cup granulated sugar
1 egg
1½ teaspoons pure vanilla extract
1¾ cups all-purpose flour
⅓ cup unsweetened cocoa powder
½ teaspoon baking powder
⅛ teaspoon salt

1 10-ounce jar maraschino cherries
   drained and cut in half,
   reserve juice

Frosting
1 cup semisweet chocolate chips
2 tablespoons reserved cherry juice

Preheat oven to 350°.

Beat butter and sugar in a large bowl with an electric mixer on medium speed until creamy. Beat in egg and vanilla extract. Add flour, cocoa powder, baking powder and salt; beat on low speed until blended. Shape dough into 1-inch balls. Place balls 1 inch apart on ungreased baking sheets.

Press a cherry half into center of each ball. Bake 8–10 minutes. Remove from oven. Cool completely before frosting.

Frosting: Cook and stir chocolate chips and cherry juice in a saucepan over low heat until chocolate is melted and smooth. Frost cooled cookies.

Makes about 3 dozen.

NO-BAKE PEANUT BUTTER CHOCOLATE CHERRY COOKIES

Chill cookies well before serving...if you can wait!

¼ **cup butter, softened**
1 **cup powdered sugar**
1 **cup peanut butter**

1⅓ **cups crisp rice cereal**
½ **cup maraschino cherries, drained, dried on paper towels**
   and chopped
6 **tablespoons mini semisweet chocolate chips**
¼ **cup chopped pecans**

1–2 **cups flaked coconut (for rolling)**

Beat butter, sugar and peanut butter in a large bowl until blended.

Stir in rice cereal, cherries, chocolate chips and pecans. Mix well.

Shape teaspoonfuls of mixture into 1-inch balls; roll in coconut. Place on waxed paper-lined baking sheets. Refrigerate and chill at least 1 hour. Store in refrigerator.

Makes about 3 dozen.

OATMEAL CHOCOLATE CHERRY DROPS

Chocolate chips and cherries in this oatmeal cookie.

1 cup butter, softened
¾ cup granulated sugar
½ cup brown sugar, packed
2 eggs
1½ teaspoons pure vanilla extract

1⅔ cups all-purpose flour
1 teaspoon baking soda
¼ teaspoon salt
2 cups uncooked old-fashioned oats
1½ cups semisweet chocolate chips
1 cup dried tart cherries, coarsely chopped

Topping
2 cups powdered sugar
2 teaspoons apple juice
2–3 tablespoons water

Preheat oven to 350°.

Beat butter, granulated sugar and brown sugar in a large bowl on medium speed with an electric mixer until creamy. Add eggs and vanilla; beat until well blended.

Add flour, baking soda and salt to bowl; beat on low speed until mixed. Stir in oats, chocolate chips and cherries by hand. Drop by rounded teaspoonfuls 2 inches apart onto ungreased baking sheets. Bake 10–12 minutes or until golden. Cool completely.

Topping; Mix all ingredients in a small bowl to a drizzling consistency. Drizzle over cooled cookies.

Makes 5 dozen.

TRIPLE CHOCOLATE CHERRY COOKIES

Lots of chocolate in these cherry cookies...use white chocolate chips with cocoa butter listed in the ingredients for best flavor.

1 cup butter, softened
1 cup granulated sugar
1 egg
1 teaspoon pure vanilla extract

1 cup semisweet chocolate chips
1 cup white chocolate chips
1 cup dried cherries

1 cup all-purpose flour
¼ cup unsweetened cocoa powder
1 teaspoon baking powder
¼ teaspoon salt

Preheat oven to 350°.

Beat butter and sugar in a large bowl with an electric mixer on medium speed until fluffy. Beat in egg and vanilla extract until blended.

Mix flour, cocoa powder, baking powder and salt in a small bowl; add to first mixture in large bowl. Beat on low speed until just blended.

Stir in chocolate chips and cherries by hand.

Drop batter by heaping teaspoonfuls 2 inches apart onto parchment-lined baking sheets. Bake 10–12 minutes. Remove from oven; cool on baking sheets 2 minutes. Remove from baking sheet. Cool on a wire rack.

Makes about 3 dozen.

Beverages

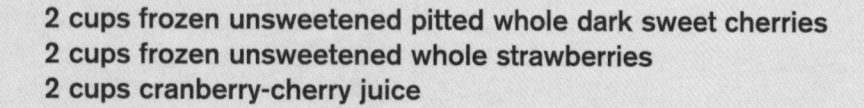

CHERRY SMOOTHIE

Share this refreshing treat with a friend.

2 cups frozen unsweetened pitted whole dark sweet cherries
2 cups frozen unsweetened whole strawberries
2 cups cranberry-cherry juice

Process all ingredients in a blender until smooth. Serve.

Makes 2 servings.

CHERRY SPICED CIDER

A mug of cider...cheers!

1 quart apple cider
¾ cup fresh orange juice
¼ cup maraschino cherry juice
1 3-inch stick cinnamon
1 fresh orange peel strip (½x3-inches)
3 whole cloves
3 whole allspice

16 maraschino cherries
8 orange slices, halved

Bring first seven ingredients to a boil in a large saucepan. Reduce heat; simmer 15 minutes. Remove from heat; strain.

To serve, add 2 maraschino cherries and 1 orange half in mugs. Fill with cider. Serve warm. Refrigerate leftovers.

Makes 6 servings.

FRESH CHERRY JUICE CONCENTRATE

Easy way to make a cool drink.

2 pounds granulated sugar
1 pound fresh sour cherries, washed and pitted
1 cup water

sparkling water

Pour sugar over cherries in a heavy saucepan; let sit 2 hours. Stir in water until sugar is dissolved.

Bring mixture to a boil. Reduce heat and simmer 15 minutes. Strain liquid into another saucepan, pressing cherries with a spoon to remove all juice; discard cherries.

Simmer liquid over low heat until mixture is syrupy and coats back of a metal spoon. Remove from heat and cool in pan. Pour syrup in a sterilized jar. Cover and store in refrigerator. To serve add 1–2 tablespoons syrup in each glass and fill glass with chilled sparkling water; stir to mix well.

Makes about 1 pint.

FRESH CHERRY SLUSH

Serve immediately.

12 fresh sweet cherries, pitted
½ cup whole fresh strawberries
½ cup cherry lemon-lime soda
1 tablespoon non-dairy whipped topping
1 tablespoon fresh lemon juice
2 ice cubes

Process all ingredients in a blender until smooth.

Makes 2 servings.

MAINEE'S CHOCOLATE CHERRY SHAKE

Just like Mainee...brown and silky smooth.

¾ cup cherry yogurt
⅔ cup maraschino cherries, drained
¾ cup whole milk
1½ cups chocolate ice cream

Process yogurt, cherries and milk in a blender until smooth. Add ice cream; process until smooth. Pour into chilled glassed. Garnish with whipping cream.

Makes 2 servings.

Breads
Muffins
Scones

ALOHA BREAD

A Hawaiian holiday treat.

1 10-ounce jar maraschino cherries, drained,
  quartered and juice reserved

⅓ cup butter or margarine, softened
⅔ cup brown sugar, packed
2 eggs
1 teaspoon pure vanilla extract

1¾ cups all-purpose flour mixed in a medium bowl with
  2 teaspoons baking powder and ½ teaspoon salt

1 cup mashed ripe bananas
½ cup chopped macadamia nuts

Preheat oven to 350°.
Lightly spray a 9x5x3-inch loaf pan with nonstick cooking spray.

Beat butter, brown sugar, eggs, vanilla and reserved cherry juice in a large bowl
with an electric mixer on medium speed until well blended.

Beat in flour mixture alternately with mashed bananas on low speed. Stir in quartered
cherries and macadamia nuts by hand. Pour batter into prepared pan; spread evenly.
Bake about 1 hour or until a wooden pick inserted in center comes out clean.
Remove from pan; cool on a wire rack. Store in refrigerator.

Makes 1 loaf.

CHOCOLATE CHERRY NUT BREAD

Chocolate and almonds in this cherry bread.

½ cup butter or margarine, softened
¾ cup brown sugar, packed
1 cup buttermilk
2 eggs
1 teaspoon pure vanilla extract

½ cup pitted dried tart cherries
½ cup semisweet miniature
   chocolate chips
⅓ cup toasted chopped
   almonds

2 cups all-purpose flour
½ teaspoon baking soda
½ teaspoon baking powder
½ teaspoon salt

Preheat oven to 350°.
Grease and flour bottom only of a 9x5-inch loaf pan.

Beat butter and sugar in a large bowl with an electric mixer on medium speed until creamy and well blended. Add buttermilk, eggs and vanilla; beat on low speed until well mixed.

Mix flour, baking soda, baking powder and salt in a small bowl; stir mixture into mixture in large bowl until just moistened. Stir in cherries, chocolate chips and almonds. Pour batter into prepared pan.

Bake 55–65 minutes or until a wooden pick inserted in center comes out clean. Remove from oven. Cool in pan 10 minutes. Remove from pan and cool completely on a wire rack. Serve or wrap and store in refrigerator.

Makes 1 loaf.

Used with permission from the Cherry Marketing Institute.

FRESH CHERRY BREAD

Serve with softened butter.

8 tablespoons butter, softened
¾ cup granulated sugar
2 eggs, beaten
1 tablespoon pure vanilla extract

1¾ cups all-purpose flour
1 tablespoon baking powder
½ teaspoon salt
½ teaspoon ground cardamom

1 cup fresh pitted cherries, chopped

Preheat oven to 350°.
Grease 9x5-inch loaf baking pan.

Beat butter and sugar in a large bowl until light and fluffy. Beat in eggs and vanilla.

Sift flour, baking powder, salt and cardamom in another bowl; stir mixture into butter mixture. Stir in cherries. Spoon batter into prepared baking pan.

Bake about 45–55 minutes or until a wooden pick inserted in center comes out clean. Remove from oven. Cool in pan 10 minutes. Remove from pan and cool on a wire rack.

Makes 1 loaf.

CHERRY CORN MUFFINS

Best served warm...with butter of course!

1¼ cups all-purpose flour
¾ cup yellow corn meal
⅔ cup dried tart cherries
½ cup granulated sugar
1 tablespoon baking powder
¼ teaspoon salt

1 cup whole milk
¼ cup corn oil
1 egg, slightly beaten
½ teaspoon pure vanilla extract

Preheat oven to 400°.
Paper line a muffin pan.

Mix first six ingredients in a medium bowl until blended.

Stir in remaining ingredients just until moistened. Spoon batter evenly into prepared pan. Bake 20–25 minutes or until a wooden pick inserted in center comes out clean. Remove from oven. Remove from pan. Serve or cool on a wire rack.

Makes 1 dozen.

Used with permission from the Cherry Marketing Institute.

PECAN SOUR CREAM CHERRY MUFFINS
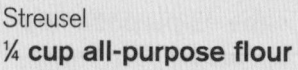

Streusel topped cherry muffins...serve warm with soft butter.

1½ cups all-purpose flour
½ cup granulated sugar
1½ teaspoons baking powder
½ teaspoon baking soda
½ teaspoon salt

Streusel
¼ cup all-purpose flour
2 tablespoons granulated sugar
¼ teaspoon ground cinnamon
1 tablespoon butter or margarine

2 eggs
⅔ cup dairy sour cream
⅛ cup corn oil
⅛ cup whole milk
½ teaspoon pure vanilla extract
1 cup dried tart cherries
½ cup coarsely chopped pecans

Preheat oven to 375°.
Grease or paper line a muffin pan.

Streusel: Mix all streusel ingredients in a small bowl until crumbly; set aside.

Mix first five ingredients in a medium bowl; set aside.

Beat eggs, sour cream, corn oil, milk and vanilla in a large bowl with an electric mixer until blended. Add flour mixture; stir until just moistened. Stir in cherries and pecans. Spoon batter evenly into prepared muffin cups. Sprinkle tops with streusel mixture. Bake 20–25 minutes or until light brown. Remove from oven. Serve or cool on a wire rack.

Makes 1 dozen.

SWEET CHERRY MUFFINS

Variation: Add ¼ cup chopped pecans.

½ cup butter, softened
1 cup granulated sugar
2 eggs
1 teaspoon pure vanilla extract
2½ cups pitted chopped sweet cherries

2 teaspoons baking powder
¼ teaspoon salt
2 cups all-purpose flour
1 cup plain yogurt

¼ cup brown sugar
1 cup sliced almonds
¼ teaspoon ground nutmeg

Preheat oven to 375°.
Generously grease 12 muffin cups.

Beat butter and sugar in a medium bowl until fluffy. Beat in eggs and vanilla extract. Stir in cherries.

Mix baking powder, salt and flour in another bowl. Stir in alternately with yogurt just until combined. Spoon batter into prepared muffin cups.

Mix brown sugar, almonds and nutmeg in a small bowl until well blended; sprinkle mixture on top of muffins.

Bake 25–30 minutes or until golden brown. Remove from oven. Cool in pan 30 minutes. Remove from pan. Refrigerate leftovers.

Makes 1 dozen.

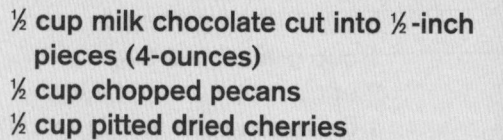

CHOCOLATE CHERRY SCONES

Chocolate lovers will enjoy these scones.

3 cups all-purpose flour
¼ cup granulated sugar
1 tablespoon baking powder
½ teaspoon salt
½ cup cold butter

¾ cup half & half (light cream)
1 large egg

½ cup milk chocolate cut into ½-inch
  pieces (4-ounces)
½ cup chopped pecans
½ cup pitted dried cherries

Preheat oven to 350°.
Butter or parchment line a 15x12-inch baking sheet.

Mix flour, sugar, baking powder and salt in a large bowl. Cut in butter with a pastry blender to form coarse crumbs.

Whisk half & half and egg in a small bowl until blended. Reserve 2 tablespoons mixture; add remaining mixture to flour mixture in bowl.

Stir in chocolate, pecans and cherries with a fork until just evenly moistened. Turn dough out onto a floured surface; with floured hands, knead dough 4 times, then squeeze dough into a ball. Pat dough out into a 7-inch round, about 1¾-inch thick. Cut into eight equal wedges. Place wedges 2-inches apart on prepared baking sheet. Brush tops lightly with reserved half & half mixture. Bake about 25 minutes or until tops are browned. Remove from oven; cool in pan 10 minutes. Serve warm. Refrigerate leftovers.

Makes 8 servings.

RUBY SCONES

Serve for breakfast or afternoon tea, with softened butter.

2 cups all-purpose flour
¼ cup granulated sugar
2 teaspoons baking powder
½ teaspoon salt
⅓ cup butter or margarine

1 cup powdered sugar
2 tablespoon fresh orange juice

1 egg, beaten
½ cup buttermilk
1 teaspoon pure vanilla extract
½ cup flaked coconut
1 teaspoon finely chopped crystallized ginger, optional
1 10-ounce jar maraschino cherries, drained and quartered

Preheat oven to 400°.
Mix flour, sugar, baking powder and salt in a large bowl. Cut in butter with a pastry blender to form coarse crumbs.

Stir in remaining ingredients, except powdered sugar and orange juice, with a fork until just combined. Knead dough on a floured surface 12 times. Pat dough out to ½-inch thickness. Cut dough into 8 pieces using a floured 4-inch round biscuit cutter. Place on an ungreased baking sheet. Cut each piece into 4 wedges with a sharp knife; do not separate. Bake 10–12 minutes or until light golden. Remove from oven.

Mix powdered sugar and orange juice in a small bowl until blended; drizzle glaze over hot scones. Serve warm. Refrigerate leftovers.

Makes 8 servings.

Used with permission from the Cherry Marketing Institute.

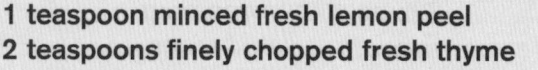

SAVORY ONION DRIED CHERRY SCONES

Cherries, lemon, thyme and yellow onion in these savory scones.

2 cups all-purpose flour
1 tablespoon granulated
  sugar
¾ teaspoon salt
2 teaspoons baking powder
6 tablespoons cold butter

1 teaspoon minced fresh lemon peel
2 teaspoons finely chopped fresh thyme
½ teaspoon coarsely ground black pepper
1 cup diced yellow onion
1¼ cups pitted dried tart cherries,
  coarsely chopped
2 eggs
½ cup heavy cream

1 egg whisked with 2 tablespoons cream
in a small bowl

Preheat oven to 425°.
Butter or parchment-line a large baking sheet.

Mix first four ingredients in a large bowl until blended. Add butter; beat with electric mixer on low until mixture is crumbly and resembles coarse meal.

Add lemon peel, thyme, black pepper, onion and cherries; beat on low until just combined. Beat in eggs and cream on low until mixture is just moistened. Turn dough out onto a floured surface. Gently knead dough, folding over itself five times. Divide dough into two equal pieces. Form each piece into a 7-inch round about ¾-inch thick. Cut each round into 6 wedges.

Brush top of wedges with egg and cream mixture. Place wedges on prepared baking sheet. Bake 20 minutes or until golden. Remove from baking sheet immediately. Cool slightly on a wire rack. Serve warm with softened butter. Refrigerate leftovers.

Makes 12 servings.

Cakes
Cheesecakes
Coffeecakes

BANANA-CHERRY CAKE

Bananas and cherries...a good combination.

1 18.25-ounce package white cake mix
3 eggs
⅓ cup corn oil
1 cup water

¼ cup fresh orange juice
¼ cup granulated sugar
1 tablespoon freshly grated orange peel
2 cups fresh or frozen dark sweet cherries
3 ripe bananas, sliced
½ teaspoon pure vanilla extract

Preheat oven to 350°.
Grease and flour a 13x9-inch baking pan.

Beat cake mix, eggs, corn oil and water in a large bowl with an electric mixer on low speed just to moisten, about 1 minute. Beat on low speed 2 minutes. Pour batter into prepared pan.

Heat orange juice, sugar and orange peel in a medium saucepan over medium heat until hot, stirring until sugar is dissolved. Add cherries; simmer until heated through. Add bananas; continue cooking 1 minute. Remove from heat. Stir in vanilla. Spoon mixture evenly over cake batter. Do not stir. Bake 35–40 minutes or until cake tests done and is lightly browned. Remove from oven. Cool in pan. Refrigerate leftovers.

Makes 16 servings.

BLACK FOREST CAKE

A homemade show stopper.

Cake
2 cups plus 2 tablespoons flour
1½ teaspoons baking powder
¾ teaspoon baking soda
¾ teaspoon salt
2 cups granulated sugar
¾ cup unsweetened cocoa powder
3 eggs
1 cup whole milk
½ cup corn oil
1 tablespoon pure vanilla extract

Frosting
3 cups whipping cream
⅓ cup powdered sugar
½ teaspoon pure vanilla extract

Topping
1 cup granulated sugar
¼ cup cornstarch
2 20-ounce cans pitted tart cherries,
  drained, reserve ½ cup juice
1 teaspoon pure vanilla extract

Preheat oven to 350°.
Grease and flour two 9-inch round baking pans; line with waxed paper.

Cake: Mix dry ingredients. Beat in eggs, milk, oil and vanilla. Divide into pans. Bake 35 minutes or until toothpick comes out clean. Cool 10 minutes; remove from pan and cool. Cut each in half horizontally. Tear one halved layer into crumbs; set aside.

Frosting: Beat all frosting ingredients with an electric mixer on high speed to stiff peaks. Reserve 1½ cups frosting; set aside.

Topping: Mix sugar and cornstarch in a saucepan. Stir in ½ cup reserved cherry juice. Add cherries; cook and stir over low heat until thickened. Stir in vanilla; cool completely.

Place one cake layer on a plate. Spread with 1 cup frosting. Top with ¾ cup topping. Repeat layers two more times. Frost side of cake with remaining frosting (not reserved frosting). Pat crumbs into frosting on side of cake. Spoon reserved frosting into a pastry bag fitted with star decorator tip. Pipe frosting around top and bottom edges of cake. Spoon remaining cherry topping onto top of cake. Store in refrigerator.

Makes 12 servings.

BLACK FOREST PUDDING CAKE

Garnish each serving with maraschino cherries as desired.

1¼ cups all-purpose flour
¾ cup granulated sugar
¼ cup unsweetened cocoa powder
1 tablespoon baking powder
½ teaspoon salt

⅔ cup whole milk
1 teaspoon pure vanilla extract
¼ cup butter, melted and slightly cooled
½ cup maraschino cherries, drained, quartered

¾ cup boiling water
½ cup chocolate syrup
¼ cup Kirsch or maraschino cherry juice

Preheat oven to 350°.
Grease an 8x8-inch square baking dish.

Mix flour, sugar, cocoa, baking powder and salt in a medium bowl.

Stir in milk, vanilla extract and butter until well mixed. Stir in cherries. Spoon batter into prepared baking dish.

Mix water, chocolate syrup and Kirsch or cherry juice in a small bowl; pour mixture evenly over batter. Bake 35–40 minutes or until center is set and edges begin to pull away from sides of baking dish. Remove from oven; let stand a few minutes before serving warm. Refrigerate leftovers.

Makes 9 servings.

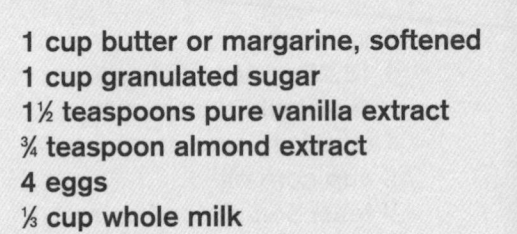

CANDIED CHERRIES BUNDT CAKE

A special cake for that holiday tray.

2 cups red candied cherries
½ cup slivered almonds

2 cups all-purpose flour, divided
2 tablespoons baking powder
1 teaspoon salt

1 cup butter or margarine, softened
1 cup granulated sugar
1½ teaspoons pure vanilla extract
¾ teaspoon almond extract
4 eggs
⅓ cup whole milk

Preheat oven to 300°.
Grease and flour a 12-cup bundt baking pan.

Mix cherries, almonds and ½ cup flour in a small bowl; set aside.

Mix remaining 1½ cups flour, baking powder and salt in another small bowl; set aside.

Beat butter and sugar with an electric mixer on medium speed until light and fluffy.
Beat in extracts. Beat in eggs, one at a time. Stir in flour mixture alternately with
milk. Fold in cherry and almond mixture. Pour batter into prepared pan.

Bake 55 minutes or until firm to touch. Remove from oven. Cool in pan 10 minutes.
Loosen cake from side of pan, and invert onto a wire rack to cool completely. Wrap
in tin foil and refrigerate several days before serving. Store in refrigerator.

Makes 12 servings.

CHERRY CHOCOLATE CAKE

Chocolate chips and maraschino cherries in this cherry-frosted cake.

Cake
- 1 18.25-ounce package moist white cake mix
- 1 cup dairy sour cream
- ½ cup corn oil
- ½ teaspoon almond extract
- ½ teaspoon pure vanilla extract
- 3 egg whites
- 1 cup miniature semisweet chocolate chips
- 1 cup chopped maraschino cherries, drained

Frosting
- 3 cups powdered sugar
- ⅓ cup butter, softened
- 1½ teaspoons pure vanilla extract
- 2 tablespoons whole milk (approximately)
- 2 tablespoons finely chopped maraschino cherries

Preheat oven to 350°.
Grease and flour a 13x9-inch baking pan

Cake: Beat cake mix, sour cream, corn oil, extracts and egg whites with an electric mixer on low speed just until moistened. Beat on medium speed 2 minutes. Stir in chocolate chips and 1 cup cherries. Spread batter into prepared pan.

Bake 25–34 minutes or until cake springs back when gently touched in center. Cool completely on a wire rack before frosting. Refrigerate leftovers.

Frosting: Mix sugar and butter in a medium bowl until blended. With an electric mixer, beat in vanilla and enough milk to form a smooth spreading consistency. Stir in 2 tablespoons chopped cherries. Add more milk if too thick. Add more sugar if too thin. Use or refrigerate.

Makes 15 servings.

CHERRY GOOD CAKE

An easy delicious scratch dessert...serve with a dollop of whipped cream.

1 cup granulated sugar
½ cup butter or margarine, softened
2 large eggs
1 teaspoon almond extract

2 cups all-purpose flour
1 teaspoon baking powder
1 teaspoon baking soda
½ teaspoon salt
1 cup dairy sour cream

1 21-ounce can cherry pie filling
½ cup sliced almonds

Preheat oven to 350°.
Grease a 13x9-inch baking pan.

Beat sugar and butter in a large bowl with an electric mixer on medium speed until well-blended, about 3 minutes. Beat in eggs and extract.

Mix flour, baking powder, baking soda and salt in a medium bowl until blended; beat mixture into butter mixture, on low speed, alternately with sour cream just until ingredients are combined; do not over beat. Spoon batter into prepared pan.

Top evenly with cherry pie filling. Sprinkle evenly with sliced almonds. Bake 35–40 minutes or until a wooden pick inserted center comes out clean. Remove from oven. Cool in pan. Refrigerate leftovers.

Makes 15 servings.

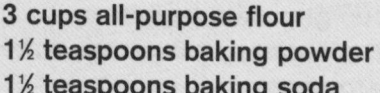

CHOCOLATE CHERRY STREUSEL CAKE

Double chocolate in this delicious homemade tart cherry cake.

1 cup brown sugar, packed
1 teaspoon ground cinnamon
½ teaspoon ground nutmeg
6 tablespoons butter, softened
1 cup semisweet chocolate chips
1 cup milk chocolate chips
½ cup rolled oats
¾ cup chopped pecans

¾ cup butter, softened
1 cup granulated sugar
3 large eggs

3 cups all-purpose flour
1½ teaspoons baking powder
1½ teaspoons baking soda
½ teaspoon salt

1⅓ cups dairy sour cream mixed in a small bowl with:
    ¾ cup dried tart cherries
    1 teaspoon freshly grated orange peel
    ¼ cup fresh orange juice
    1 teaspoon pure vanilla extract

Preheat oven to 350°.
Grease a 13x9-inch baking pan.

Streusel: Mix brown sugar, cinnamon and nutmeg. Cut in 6 tablespoons butter until crumbly. Stir in chocolate chips, oats and pecans; set aside.

Beat ¾ cup butter and 1 cup granulated sugar on medium speed 4 minutes. Beat in eggs, one at a time.

Mix flour, baking powder, baking soda and salt. Add to butter mixture alternately with sour cream mixture, beating until just combined.
Spread batter into prepared pan. Bake 20 minutes. Remove from oven; sprinkle with streusel. Return to oven; bake 15–20 minutes or until a wooden pick inserted in center comes out clean. Cool in pan on a wire rack. Refrigerate leftovers.

Makes 16 servings.

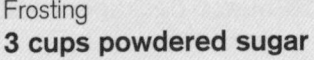

CHOCOLATE CHIP CHERRY CAKE

Double chocolate and cherry pie filling in this cake...serve plain or frost.

1 18-ounce package chocolate
   cake mix
1 21-ounce can cherry pie filling
2 large eggs
⅓ cup corn oil
1 teaspoon pure vanilla extract
1 cup semisweet chocolate chips

Frosting
3 cups powdered sugar
⅓ cup butter
1½ teaspoons pure vanilla extract
2 tablespoons whole milk
   (approximately)

Preheat oven to 350°.
Grease a 13x9-inch baking pan.

Cake: Beat cake mix, pie filling, eggs, corn oil and vanilla extract in a large bowl
with an electric mixer on low speed 30 seconds. Beat on medium speed 2 minutes.
Stir in chocolate chips. Pour batter into prepared pan.

Bake 25–30 minutes or until a wooden pick inserted in center comes out clean.
Remove from oven. Cool in pan on a wire rack. Frost. Refrigerate leftovers.

Frosting: Mix sugar and butter in a medium bowl until blended. Beat in vanilla and
just enough milk with an electric mixer to form a smooth spreading consistency.
Refrigerate leftovers.

Makes 12 servings.

FROSTED CHERRY JUBILEE CAKE

Variation: Use 1 tub of already prepared classic chocolate frosting.

1 18-ounce package moist devils food cake mix

½ cup chopped maraschino cherries
2 cups frozen non-dairy whipped topping

Frosting
3 cups powdered sugar
⅓ cup butter, softened
3 ounces unsweetened baking chocolate, melted and cooled
2 teaspoons pure vanilla extract
3 tablespoons milk (approximately)

Preheat oven to 350°.
Grease and flour two 9-inch round cake pans.

Prepare, bake and cool cake as directed on package.

Fold cherries into whipped topping in a bowl.

Place one completely cooled cake layer on a serving plate. Spread with whipped topping cherry mixture. Top with second completely cooled cake layer. Frost sides and top with chocolate frosting below. Refrigerate.

Frosting: Beat powdered sugar and butter in a medium bowl with an electric mixer on low speed until blended. Stir in chocolate and vanilla extract. Beat in enough milk to form a smooth frosting.

Makes 12 servings.

HUMMINGBIRD CAKE

Cherry buttercream frosting on this good cake...funny name!

Cake
1 18.25 package moist yellow cake mix
3 eggs
⅓ cup corn oil
1 8-ounce can crushed pineapple,
    drained, reserve juice
⅓ cup reserved pineapple juice (add
    water if necessary to make ⅓ cup)
2 ripe medium size bananas, mashed
1 teaspoon ground cinnamon
1 teaspoon pure vanilla extract
½ cup finely chopped pecans
½ cup chopped maraschino cherries, drained

Cherry buttercream frosting
3 cups powdered sugar
⅓ cup butter, softened
1½ teaspoons pure vanilla
    extract
2 tablespoons milk
    (approximately)
2 tablespoons chopped
    maraschino cherries,
    drained

Preheat oven to 350°.
Grease bottom and flour a 13x9-inch baking pan.

Cake: Beat cake mix, eggs, corn oil, pineapple, pineapple juice, bananas, cinnamon and vanilla extract in a large bowl with an electric mixer on low speed 2 minutes. Stir in pecans and cherries. Pour batter into prepared pan. Bake 30–35 minutes or until cake springs back when touched in center. Remove from oven. Cool completely in pan. Frost. Store in refrigerator.

Cherry buttercream frosting: Beat powdered sugar and butter in a medium bowl with an electric mixer until smooth. Beat in 1½ teaspoons vanilla extract and milk until smooth. Stir in cherries by hand. Spread on cooled cake. Refrigerate leftovers.

Makes 15 servings.

KIKI'S CHERRY CHOCOLATE CAKE

Karan, a long-time friend, better know as Grandma Kiki, from
Blaine, Minnesota, shares a quick-to-prepare cake recipe.

1 18.25-ounce package chocolate
   cake mix
2 eggs
⅓ cup corn oil
1 teaspoon pure vanilla extract
1 21-ounce can cherry pie filling

Frosting
1 cup granulated sugar
⅓ cup whole milk
5 tablespoons butter
1 6-ounce package
   semisweet chocolate chips

Preheat oven to 350°.
Grease and flour a 13x9-inch baking pan.

Beat first 4 ingredients in a large bowl with an electric mixer on medium speed 1
minute. Stir in cherry pie filling until well blended. Pour mixture into prepared pan.
Bake 30–35 minutes or until a wooden pick inserted in center comes out clean.
Remove from oven.

Frosting: Bring sugar and milk to a boil over medium heat in a medium saucepan.
Stir in butter; bring to a boil stirring constantly. Boil for 1 minute. Remove from
heat; stir in chocolate chips until melted. Immediately pour mixture over cake.
Refrigerate leftovers.

Makes 15 servings.

MARASCHINO OATMEAL CAKE

Moist and delicious...serve warm or cool with sweetened whipped cream. Garnish with stemmed maraschino cherries as desired.

Cake
1¼ cups boiling water
1 cup uncooked old-fashioned oats
¾ cup granulated sugar
½ cup butter, softened
2 eggs
2 cups all-purpose flour
1 teaspoon baking soda
1 teaspoon salt
1 teaspoon pure vanilla extract
1 10-ounce jar maraschino cherries, drained and chopped

Topping
1¼ cups flaked coconut
½ cup brown sugar, packed
⅓ cup butter, melted
⅓ cup whipping cream

Preheat oven to 350°.
Grease and flour a 13x9-inch baking pan.

Cake: Stir boiling water and oats in a medium bowl; set aside. Beat granulated sugar, brown sugar and butter in a large bowl with an electric mixer on medium speed until well mixed. Beat in eggs until well blended, about 2 minutes. Mix flour, baking soda and salt in a small bowl; add to mixture in large bowl. Add vanilla extract and oat mixture. Beat on low speed until well mixed. Stir in cherries by hand. Pour batter into prepared pan. Bake 30–35 minutes or until a wooden pick inserted in center comes out clean. Remove from oven. Turn on broiler.

Topping: Mix all topping ingredients in a medium bowl. Spread mixture over hot cake. Broil 4–5 inches from broiler heat until bubbly and lightly browned, about 3 minutes (do not let burn).

Makes 15 servings.

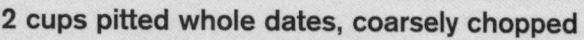

MINI CHERRY FRUIT CAKES

Line the holiday buffet table with these little fruitcakes.

2 cups pitted whole dates, coarsely chopped
2 cups dried apricot halves, coarsely chopped
1 cup Brazil nuts, coarsely chopped
½ cup coarsely chopped pecans
1 cup candied pineapple, chopped
1 cup red and green whole maraschino cherries, drained

¾ cup all purpose flour
¾ cup granulated sugar
½ teaspoon baking powder
½ teaspoon salt
2 teaspoons pure vanilla extract
3 large eggs

melted apricot preserves

Preheat oven to 300°.
Paper or foil line 24 medium muffin cups.

Mix first 6 ingredients in a large bowl.

Combine flour, sugar, baking powder and salt in another small bowl; add to large bowl mixture. Add vanilla extract and eggs. Stir until well mixed. Spoon batter equally into muffin cups (about ⅓ cup each). Bake 35–40 minutes or until a wooden pick inserted in center comes out clean.

Remove from pan to a wire rack; brush tops with melted apricot preserves. Store tightly wrapped in refrigerator.

Makes 24 servings.

BLACK FOREST CHOCOLATE CHEESECAKE

Black forest cheesecake...always a favorite with chocolate lovers.

Crust
1½ cups chocolate cookie crumbs
3 tablespoons butter, melted

Filling
2 1-ounce squares unsweetened
   baking chocolate
1 14-ounce can sweetened condensed milk
2 8-ounce packages cream cheese, softened
3 eggs
3 tablespoons cornstarch
1 teaspoon almond extract

Topping
1 21-ounce can cherry pie
   filling, chilled
sweetened whipped cream

Preheat oven to 300°.

Crust: Mix cookie crumbs and butter in a small bowl. Press mixture onto bottom of an ungreased 9-inch springform baking pan.

Filling: Heat chocolate and sweetened condensed milk, stirring constantly, in a small saucepan over low heat until chocolate is melted. Remove from heat; set aside. Beat cream cheese in a large bowl until fluffy. Gradually beat in chocolate mixture until smooth. Beat in eggs, cornstarch and almond extract. Pour mixture into prepared pan. Bake about 55 minutes or until center is set. Cool to room temperature, then refrigerate. Chill well. Remove side of pan.

Topping: Top with cherry pie filling. Garnish each serving with sweetened whipped cream. Refrigerate leftovers.

Makes 10 servings.

CHERRIES JUBILEE CHEESECAKE

Garnish each serving with whipped cream when serving.

Crust
1¼ cups graham cracker crumbs
¼ cup granulated sugar
⅓ cup butter, melted

Topping
2 teaspoons cornstarch
1 tablespoon granulated sugar

Filling
3 8-ounce packages cream cheese, softened
1 14-ounce can sweetened condensed milk
4 eggs
¼ cup kirsch or other cherry-flavored liqueur, divided
1½ teaspoons almond extract, divided
1 17-ounce can pitted dark sweet cherries, divided, drained,
   reserve syrup
1 tablespoon all-purpose flour

Preheat oven to 300°.
Crust: Mix all crust ingredients; press firmly on bottom of an ungreased 9-inch springform pan.

Filling: Beat cream cheese until fluffy. Gradually beat in sweetened condensed milk until smooth. Add eggs, 3 tablespoons kirsch and 1 teaspoon almond extract. Chop ½ cup cherries; toss with flour and stir into mixture. Pour into pan. Bake 70 minutes or until center is set. Cool and refrigerate. Remove side of pan just before serving.

Topping: Mix cornstarch and sugar in a small saucepan. Stir in reserved cherry syrup, 1 tablespoon kirsch and ½ teaspoon almond extract. Cook and stir over medium heat until thickened. Cool. Cut remaining cherries in half; stir into sauce. Chill. Spoon over cheesecake when serving. Refrigerate leftovers.

Makes 12 servings.

CHERRY-SWIRLED CHEESECAKE

Variation: Use chocolate cookie crumbs instead of graham crackers.

Crust
- ½ **cup sliced almonds, toasted and finely chopped**
- 1¼ **cups graham cracker crumbs**
- ¼ **cup granulated sugar**
- ⅓ **cup butter, melted**

Filling
- 1 **21-ounce can cherry pie filling**
- 1 **teaspoon grated fresh orange peel**
- 2 **8-ounce packages cream cheese, softened**
- 1 **14-ounce can sweetened condensed milk**
- 3 **eggs**
- ⅓ **cup lemon juice**
- 1 **teaspoon pure vanilla extract**

Preheat oven to 325°.
Crust: Mix all crust ingredients in a small bowl; press mixture on bottom of an ungreased 9-inch springform baking pan.

Filling: Puree pie filling in a blender until smooth; pour mixture into a small bowl. Stir in grated orange peel; refrigerate.

Beat cream cheese in a large bowl with an electric mixer until fluffy. Gradually beat in sweetened condensed milk until smooth. Beat in eggs, lemon juice and vanilla until well mixed. Pour half the batter into prepared crust. Top with ½ cup puree mixture; repeat layering. Carefully swirl puree mixture with a knife into cream cheese mixture.

Bake 50–55 minutes or until center is set. Remove from oven. Cool in pan, then refrigerate. Chill well. Run a knife around side of pan to loosen cheesecake. Remove side of pan. Serve topped with remaining puree mixture and whipped cream. Store in refrigerator.

Makes 12 servings.

Used with permission from the Cherry Marketing Institute.

CHERRY-TOPPED CHEESECAKE

Classic cheesecake...serve with a dollop of whipped cream.

Crust
1¾ cups graham cracker crumbs
¼ cup granulated sugar
⅓ cup butter, melted

Filling
3 8-ounce packages cream cheese, softened
1 cup granulated sugar
3 eggs
1 cup dairy sour cream
2 teaspoons pure vanilla extract

Topping
1 21-ounce can cherry pie filling

Preheat oven to 350°.

Crust: Mix all crust ingredients in a bowl; press mixture onto bottom and 2½ inches up side of a 9-inch springform baking pan; set aside.

Filling: Beat cream cheese and sugar with an electric mixer on high speed until well blended. Beat in eggs on low speed, one at a time. Add sour cream and vanilla; beat on low speed until blended. Pour mixture into prepared crust.

Bake 60–70 minutes or until center is almost set. Turn oven off. Leave door slightly ajar, and leave cheesecake in oven 1 hour. Remove from oven. Cool completely in pan on a wire rack, then refrigerate. Chill well. Remove side of pan.

Top with cherry pie filling. Refrigerate leftovers.

Makes 16 servings.

FRESH CHERRY CHEESECAKE

A chocolate-almond crust holds this fresh cherry cheesecake.

Crust
1 cup whole almonds, blanched, lightly toasted
20 thin chocolate wafer cookies
¼ cup butter, softened
⅓ cup granulated sugar
¼ teaspoon salt
½ teaspoon pure vanilla extract

Filling
2 8-ounce packages cream cheese, softened
1 cup granulated sugar
3 large eggs
3 tablespoons all-purpose flour
1 8-ounce container dairy sour cream
3 tablespoons whipping cream
2 teaspoons pure vanilla extract

Topping
¾ teaspoon unflavored gelatin
1 tablespoon cold water
3 cups stemmed and pitted fresh tart cherries
6 tablespoons granulated sugar
1 tablespoon fresh lemon juice
½ teaspoon pure vanilla extract

Preheat oven to 350°.

Crust: Process almonds in food processor. Add wafers; grind fine. Add butter, sugar, salt and vanilla; process until well combined. Press onto bottom and 1 inch up side of a 9-inch springform baking pan. Bake 10 minutes. Cool on a wire rack.
Filling: Beat cream cheese and sugar with an electric mixer on medium speed until smooth. Beat in eggs, one at a time. Beat in flour, sour cream, whipping cream and vanilla. Pour into crust. Bake 50 minutes or until almost, but not completely set. Cool in pan on a wire rack. Refrigerate 1 hour. Remove side of pan. Place on a serving plate; spread with topping. Chill well before serving. Refrigerate leftovers.
Topping: Sprinkle gelatin over water; let soften, about 1 minute. Bring cherries, sugar and lemon juice to a boil, stirring constantly. Remove from heat. Stir in gelatin mixture until dissolved. Stir in vanilla.

Makes 12 servings.

MARASCHINO-TOPPED MALLOW CHEESECAKE

Marshmallows in this creamy no-bake cheesecake...topped with maraschino cherries and toasted pecans.

Crust
1 cup vanilla wafer crumbs
¼ cup butter or margarine, melted

Filling
4 cups miniature marshmallows
⅓ cup fresh orange juice
2 8-ounce packages cream cheese, softened
1 teaspoon pure vanilla extract
1 cup whipping cream, whipped

Topping
24 whole stemmed maraschino cherries, halved
24 toasted pecan halves

Preheat oven to 325°.

Crust: Mix vanilla wafer crumbs and butter in a small bowl; press onto bottom of an ungreased 9-inch springform baking pan. Bake 10 minutes. Remove from oven. Cool.

Filling: Stir marshmallows and orange juice in a medium saucepan over low heat until marshmallows are melted and mixture is smooth. Chill until slightly thickened, then mix until well blended. Beat cream cheese and vanilla extract in a large bowl with an electric mixer until smooth. Add chilled marshmallow mixture; mix well. Fold in whipped cream. Pour mixture into prepared crust. Chill well. Remove side of pan.

Top with cherries and pecans. Refrigerate leftovers.

Makes 12 servings.

THE GIRLS' CHERRY CHEESECAKE

Cookie-crusted cherry cheesecake...the girls purr for this treat.

Crust
1 18-ounce roll refrigerated sugar slice and bake cookies

Filling
2 8-ounce packages cream cheese, softened
1 cup dairy sour cream
¾ cup granulated sugar
1 teaspoon pure vanilla extract
3 eggs
1 21-ounce can cherry pie filling

Preheat oven to 350°.
Grease a 9-inch springform baking pan.

Crust: Cut cookie dough into ⅛-inch slices and arrange slightly overlapping onto bottom and sides of pan. Press edges to form crust.

Filling: Beat cream cheese in a large bowl with an electric mixer until fluffy. Beat in sour cream, sugar and vanilla extract until well blended. Beat in eggs until blended. Reserve ¼ cup mixture; set aside. Pour remaining mixture into prepared crust. Bake 70 minutes.

Increase temperature to 450°.
Spoon cherry pie filling evenly over cheesecake. Top with reserved ¼ cup mixture; swirl lightly with a fork to create an interesting pattern. Bake 10 minutes. Remove from oven. Loosen cake from side of pan with a thin knife. Cool; remove side of pan and refrigerate. Serve chilled. Garnish with whipped cream if desired. Refrigerate leftovers.

Makes 12 servings.

WHITE CHOCOLATE CHEESECAKE

Delicious and simple to prepare.

Crust
1 cup pecan halves, lightly toasted, divided
1½ cups graham cracker crumbs
¼ cup granulated sugar
¼ cup butter, melted

Filling
3 8-ounce packages cream cheese, softened
1 14-ounce can sweetened condensed milk
1 teaspoon pure vanilla extract
1 6-ounce package *white baking chocolate, melted
4 eggs

Topping
1 21 ounce can cherry pie filling
1 teaspoon pure vanilla extract
1 cup frozen non-dairy whipped topping, thawed
reserved pecan halves

Preheat oven to 300°.

Crust: Reserve 16 pecan halves for topping. Finely chop remaining pecans; mix with cracker crumbs, sugar and butter until blended. Press mixture onto bottom of an ungreased 9-inch springform baking pan; set aside.

Filling: Beat cream cheese on medium speed until creamy. Beat in milk and vanilla. Beat in chocolate on low speed. Beat in eggs, one at a time on low speed just until blended. Pour into prepared crust. Bake 1 hour or until center is almost set. Loosen cake from side of pan. Cool in pan, then remove side of pan. Store in refrigerator. Chill 4 hours before serving.

Topping: Mix pie filling and vanilla; spoon over chilled cheesecake. Top with whipped topping. Garnish with pecan halves. Refrigerate leftovers.

Makes 16 servings.

*Select white chocolate with cocoa butter for best flavor.

ALMOND CHERRY CREAM CHEESE COFFEECAKE

Serve warm or cool. Garnish with whipped cream, if desired.

1 18.25-ounce package moist white cake mix
¼ cup dairy sour cream
1 teaspoon almond extract
2 eggs, divided

1 8-ounce package cream cheese, softened
¼ cup granulated sugar
½ cup cherry preserves
½ cup sliced almonds

Preheat oven to 350°.
Grease a 9x9-inch baking pan.

Beat cake mix, sour cream, almond extract and 1 egg with an electric mixer on low speed until crumbly. Reserve ½ cup crumb mixture. Press remaining crumb mixture in bottom and 1 inch up side of prepared pan. Bake until light golden, about 18 minutes. Remove from oven.

Beat cream cheese, sugar and 1 egg with an electric mixer on medium speed until smooth. Pour over baked crust. Drop cherry preserves by teaspoonfuls evenly over cream cheese; do not mix.

Mix reserved crumb mixture with almonds; sprinkle evenly over cherry preserves. Return to oven. Bake 25–30 minutes or until filling is set. Cool slightly before cutting into squares. Store in refrigerator.

Makes 16 servings.

CHERRY SWIRL COFFEECAKE

All you need now is a steaming cup of your favorite coffee.

1 18.25-ounce moist white cake mix
½ cup dairy sour cream
⅓ cup butter, softened
1 teaspoon pure vanilla extract
2 eggs
1 21-ounce can cherry pie filling

Glaze
1 cup powdered sugar
2 tablespoons cherry juice or fresh orange juice (approximately)
½ teaspoon pure vanilla extract

Preheat oven to 350°.
Grease a 15x10x1-inch jelly roll baking pan.

Coffeecake: Mix dry cake mix, sour cream, butter, vanilla and eggs with a spoon in a large bowl to form soft dough. Reserve 1 cup. Spread remaining dough in prepared pan. Spoon cherry pie filling over dough; spread evenly. Drop reserved 1 cup dough by spoonfuls evenly over pie filling.

Bake 25 minutes or until a wooden pick inserted in center comes out clean. Remove from oven. Drizzle warm cake with glaze. Cool slightly before cutting into serving pieces. Serve warm. Store in refrigerator.

Glaze: Stir all glaze ingredients in a small bowl to form a smooth drizzling consistency. Add more sugar if too thick, add more juice if too thin.

Makes 15 servings.

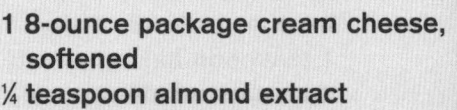

CREAM CHEESE CHERRY COFFEECAKE

Serve this yummy coffeecake for that special breakfast or brunch.

1½ cups all-purpose flour
1 cup rolled oats
1 cup granulated sugar, divided
¾ cup cold butter or margarine
½ cup dairy sour cream
2 eggs, divided
½ teaspoon baking soda

1 8-ounce package cream cheese, softened
¼ teaspoon almond extract
¾ cup cherry pie filling
⅓ cup sliced almonds

Preheat oven to 350°.
Grease a 9-inch springform baking pan.

Mix flour, oats and ¾ cup sugar in a large bowl; cut in butter until coarse crumbs form. Remove 1 cup crumb mixture; set aside. Add sour cream, 1 egg and baking soda to remaining crumbly mixture in bowl; stir well. Spread mixture onto bottom and 2-inches up side of prepared pan.

Beat cream cheese, ¼ cup sugar and almond extract in a medium bowl with an electric mixer on medium speed until well blended. Beat in 1 egg on low speed until blended. Spoon mixture into prepared crust. Top with cherry pie filling. Sprinkle with 1 cup reserved crumb mixture, then sprinkle evenly with sliced almonds.

Bake 50–55 minutes or until golden. Remove from oven; cool in pan 15 minutes. Loosen cake with a knife around side of pan. Remove side. Serve warm or at room temperature. Refrigerate leftovers.

Makes 16 servings.

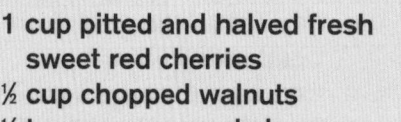

FRESH CHERRY COFFEECAKE

Sour cream and walnuts in this fresh cherry coffeecake.

2½ cups all-purpose flour
1 teaspoon baking powder
½ teaspoon baking soda

1 cup butter, softened
1¼ cups granulated sugar
1 teaspoon pure vanilla extract
½ teaspoon freshly grated lemon rind
2 large eggs
1 cup dairy sour cream

1 cup pitted and halved fresh
   sweet red cherries
½ cup chopped walnuts
½ teaspoon ground cinnamon
2 tablespoons granulated sugar

Topping
1 tablespoon sugar
¼ teaspoon cinnamon

Preheat oven to 350°.
Grease and flour a 9-inch tube baking pan.

Mix flour, baking powder and baking soda in a medium bowl.

Beat butter and 1¼ cups sugar in a large bowl until creamy. Beat in vanilla extract and lemon rind. Beat in eggs, one at a time. Gradually beat in flour mixture alternately with sour cream until well blended.

Mix cherries, walnuts, ½ teaspoon ground cinnamon and 2 tablespoons sugar in a small bowl.

Topping: Mix topping ingredients in a cup.

Spoon a third of the batter into prepared baking pan. Sprinkle with half of the cherry mixture. Repeat layers ending with batter. Sprinkle with topping. Bake about 1 hour or until a wooden pick inserted in center comes out clean. Cool 5 minutes in pan before removing to a wire rack.

Makes 12 servings.

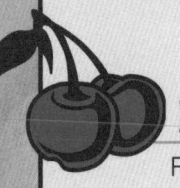

PECAN CHERRY COFFEECAKE

Pecans and sour cream in this delicious cherry coffeecake.

Coffeecake
1 cup granulated sugar
¾ cup butter, softened
1 cup dairy sour cream
2 eggs
1 teaspoon pure vanilla extract
2 cups all-purpose flour
1½ teaspoons baking powder
½ teaspoon baking soda
½ teaspoon salt
1 21-ounce can cherry pie filling

Topping
¼ cup granulated sugar
¼ cup all-purpose flour
½ cup chopped pecans
1 teaspoon ground cinnamon
3 tablespoons butter

Preheat oven to 325°.
Grease and flour a 13x9-inch baking pan.

Coffeecake: Mix sugar and softened butter in a large bowl. Beat with an electric mixer on medium speed until creamy. Add sour cream, eggs and vanilla extract. Beat until well mixed. Mix flour, baking powder, baking soda and salt in a small bowl; add to creamy mixture; beat on low speed until well mixed. Spread half of batter into prepared pan. Spoon cherry filling over batter. Spread remaining batter carefully over pie filling.

Topping: Mix sugar, flour, pecans and cinnamon in a medium bowl. Cut in butter until crumbly. Sprinkle mixture over batter. Bake 45–50 minutes or until a wooden pick inserted in center comes out clean. Remove from oven. Serve warm. Refrigerate leftovers.

Makes 15 servings.

Cobblers
Crisps

APRICOT-CHERRY COBBLER

Substitute two pounds frozen sweet cherries, thawed and drained.

2 pounds fresh Bing cherries,
   pitted
2 pounds fresh apricots,
   halved and pitted
1 cup granulated sugar
3 tablespoons cornstarch
1 teaspoon almond extract

Topping
2½ cups all-purpose flour
½ cup granulated sugar
1½ teaspoons baking powder
¾ teaspoon baking soda
½ teaspoon salt
½ cup cold butter, cut into ½-inch cubes
¾ cup buttermilk
¾ cup whipping cream
1 tablespoon granulated sugar

Preheat oven to 400°.

Mix first 5 ingredients until blended. Spoon mixture into an ungreased 13x9-inch glass baking dish. Bake about 35 minutes or until filling begins to bubble at edges. Remove from oven.

Reduce heat to 375°.

Topping: Mix flour, ½ cup sugar, baking powder, baking soda and salt until blended. Cut in butter until mixture resembles coarse meal. Gradually add buttermilk and whipping cream, tossing with a fork until dough is formed. Drop dough by rounded tablespoonfuls over hot filling to cover. Sprinkle with 1 tablespoon sugar. Return to oven and continue baking 35–40 minutes or until a wooden pick inserted in center of topping comes out clean. Remove from oven; cool slightly before serving with ice cream. Refrigerate leftovers.

Makes 12 servings.

CHERRY COBBLER

Pretty quick...tasty too. Serve warm with ice cream.

1 21-ounce can cherry pie filling
½ teaspoon pure vanilla extract

1 cup all-purpose baking mix
¼ cup whole milk
1 tablespoon granulated sugar
1 tablespoon butter, softened

Preheat oven to 400°.

Spoon pie filling into an ungreased 1½-quart baking dish. Stir in vanilla.
Bake 10 minutes. Remove from oven.

Mix remaining ingredients in a bowl to form soft dough. Drop dough by 6 large
spoonfuls on top of hot pie filling. Return to oven; bake until topping is light brown,
about 20 minutes. Refrigerate leftovers.

Makes 6 servings.

MARY DOW'S CHERRY COBBLER

Top with whipped cream when serving.

1 21-ounce can cherry pie filling
1 15-ounce can pitted dark sweet cherries, drained
2 tablespoons butter

1 8-ounce package cream cheese, softened
⅓ cup granulated sugar
⅓ cup all-purpose flour
1 large egg
1½ teaspoons pure vanilla extract

20 vanilla wafers, crushed
2 tablespoons butter, melted

Preheat oven to 350°.
Lightly butter a 9-inch deep-dish pie plate.

Stir cherry pie filling, dark sweet cherries and 2 tablespoons butter in a large saucepan over medium heat until completely heated, about 5 minutes. Spoon hot mixture into prepared pie plate.

Beat cream cheese, sugar and flour in a bowl until blended. Beat in egg and vanilla extract until smooth. Spoon mixture over hot cherry mixture.

Mix vanilla wafers and 2 tablespoons melted butter in a bowl; sprinkle over cream cheese layer. Bake until filling is set, about 30 minutes. Remove from oven. Cool slightly before serving. Store in refrigerator.

Makes 8 servings.

ORANGE-CHERRY COBBLER

Serve warm...top with ice cream if desired.

2 21-ounce cans cherry pie filling
1 teaspoon vanilla extract

1 cup all-purpose flour
2 tablespoons granulated sugar
2 teaspoons baking powder
⅛ teaspoon salt
½ cup fresh orange juice

1 tablespoon slivered almonds, chopped
1 tablespoon granulated sugar
1 teaspoon freshly grated orange peel
½ teaspoon ground cinnamon

Preheat oven to 350°.

Mix pie filling and vanilla extract in an ungreased 8x8-inch baking pan.

Mix flour, 2 tablespoons sugar, baking powder and salt in a medium bowl until blended. Add orange juice; stir just until moistened. Drop batter by tablespoonfuls over pie filling.

Mix almonds, 1 tablespoon sugar, orange peel and cinnamon in a small bowl; sprinkle over all. Bake 30–35 minutes or until filling is bubbly and topping browned. Refrigerate leftovers.

Makes 8 servings.

PEACHY FRESH CHERRY COBBLER

Serve with vanilla ice cream.

6 cups fresh peaches, peeled and sliced
4 cups fresh pitted sweet cherries
¾ cup granulated sugar
¼ cup cornstarch
3 tablespoons fresh lemon juice
½ teaspoon pure vanilla extract

Biscuits
2 cups all-purpose flour
⅓ cup granulated sugar
2½ teaspoons baking powder
½ teaspoon salt
½ cup butter, cut into pieces
¾ cup heavy cream

Topping
2 tablespoons granulated sugar
2 tablespoons heavy cream
¼ teaspoon ground cinnamon

Preheat oven to 425°.
Grease a 13x9-inch glass baking dish.

Mix peaches, cherries, ¾ cup sugar and cornstarch in a large saucepan. Bring to a boil, stirring often over high heat; boil 1 minute. Remove from heat; stir in lemon juice and vanilla. Spoon into prepared baking dish.

Biscuits: Mix flour, ⅓ cup sugar, baking powder and salt in a large bowl. Cut in butter with a pastry blender until crumbly. Stir in cream. Knead just until dough holds together. Roll out on a floured surface to ½-inch thick. Cut with a 3-inch biscuit cutter. Place biscuits over fruit mixture.

Topping: Mix ingredients in a cup; brush over biscuits. Bake until fruit is bubbly, about 20 minutes. Remove from oven; let stand 10 minutes. Refrigerate leftovers.

Makes 10 servings.

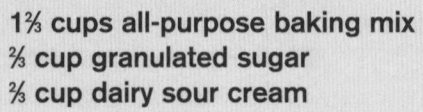

SOUR CREAM CHERRY COBBLER

Sour cream makes the batter better for this sweet cherry crisp.

1⅔ cups all-purpose baking mix
⅔ cup granulated sugar
⅔ cup dairy sour cream
⅛ cup whole milk
¼ teaspoon almond extract

1 21-ounce can cherry pie filling

**¼ cup sliced almonds mixed in a small bowl with 1 tablespoon
granulated sugar and a pinch of ground nutmeg**

Preheat oven to 375°.
Spray a 9x9-inch baking pan with nonstick cooking spray.

Mix first five ingredients in a medium bowl until smooth. Spread batter evenly into
prepared pan.

Spoon pie filling evenly over batter. Bake 35–40 minutes or until golden. Remove
from oven.

Sprinkle almond mixture over partially baked cobbler. Return to oven and bake
10–20 minutes or until a wooden pick inserted in center comes out clean. Serve
warm with vanilla ice cream. Refrigerate leftovers.

Makes 6 servings.

BLUEBERRY-CHERRY CRISP

Cake mix is used for topping in this good crisp.

1 21-ounce can blueberry pie filling
1 21-ounce can cherry pie filling
1 tablespoon fresh lemon juice
1 teaspoon pure vanilla extract

1 18.25-ounce package moist yellow cake mix
½ cup butter, melted and cooled
½ cup chopped pecans

Preheat oven to 350°.

Spoon pie fillings into a 13x9-inch ungreased baking pan. Do not mix. Sprinkle with lemon juice and vanilla extract over top.

Mix dry cake mix, butter and pecans in a large bowl with a spoon until crumbly. Sprinkle evenly over pie fillings. Bake 35–40 minutes or until golden. Serve warm with vanilla ice cream. Refrigerate leftovers.

Makes 12 servings.

CHOCOLATE CHERRY CRISP

Serve this quick dessert with a dollop of sweetened whipped cream.

1 21-ounce can cherry pie filling
1 teaspoon pure vanilla extract

½ cup all-purpose baking mix
½ cup uncooked quick-cooking oats
½ cup brown sugar, packed
¼ cup chilled butter
½ cup semisweet chocolate chips

Preheat oven to 350°.

Spoon pie filling into an 8x8-inch ungreased baking dish. Stir in vanilla; spread evenly.

Mix baking mix, oats and brown sugar in a bowl. Cut in butter with a pastry blender until crumbly. Stir in chocolate chips. Sprinkle mixture evenly over pie filling. Bake 30–35 minutes or until bubbly and lightly browned. Serve warm. Refrigerate leftovers.

Makes 8 servings.

COCONUT CHERRY CRISP

Substitute frozen unsweetened pitted tart cherries; thaw, but do not drain.

¼ cup granulated sugar
4 teaspoons cornstarch
5 cups fresh tart red cherries, pitted
2 tablespoons cold water

¾ cup rolled oats
½ cup brown sugar, packed
⅓ cup all-purpose flour
¼ teaspoon ground nutmeg
⅓ cup butter
½ cup flaked coconut
¼ cup chopped pecans

Preheat oven to 375°.
Lightly butter a 2-quart square baking dish.

Mix sugar and cornstarch in a large saucepan. Stir in cherries and water. Cook and stir over medium heat until bubbly and is thickened. Pour mixture into prepared baking dish.

Mix oats, brown sugar, flour and nutmeg in a medium bowl. Cut in butter until crumbly. Stir in coconut and pecans. Sprinkle over filling. Bake about 25 minutes or until golden. Serve warm with vanilla ice cream. Refrigerate leftovers.

Makes 6 servings.

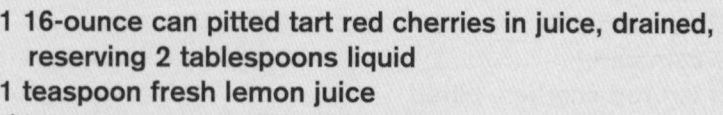

COOKIE CRUST CHERRY CRISP

Vanilla wafers top this cherry crisp.

**1 16-ounce can pitted tart red cherries in juice, drained,
  reserving 2 tablespoons liquid**
1 teaspoon fresh lemon juice
½ teaspoon pure vanilla extract
2 drops red food coloring, optional

⅓ cup granulated sugar
½ teaspoon ground cinnamon
1½ cups vanilla wafer cookie crumbs
⅓ cup melted butter

Preheat oven to 400°.
Lightly butter bottom of an 8x8-inch baking dish.

Mix cherries, 2 tablespoons reserved cherry liquid, lemon juice, vanilla extract and
food coloring in a medium bowl. Pour mixture into prepared baking dish.

Mix granulated sugar and cinnamon in a small dish; sprinkle over cherry mixture.
Mix cookie crumbs and melted butter in a small bowl; sprinkle over cherries, then
pat down slightly. Bake 25 minutes. Serve warm with a dollop of whipped topping.
Refrigerate leftovers.

Makes 6 servings.

NECTARINE-CHERRY CRISP

Fresh fruit in this good crisp...serve warm with vanilla ice cream.

3 pounds ripe nectarines, each cut into 6 wedges
1½ pounds dark sweet cherries, stemmed and pitted
2 tablespoons fresh lemon juice
½ cup granulated sugar mixed in a small bowl
   with 3 tablespoons cornstarch
2 tablespoons cold butter, cut up

Topping
⅔ cup brown sugar, packed
6 tablespoons butter, softened
1 large egg
2 teaspoons pure vanilla extract
1½ cups rolled oats
¾ cup all-purpose flour
¼ teaspoon salt
¼ teaspoon baking soda

Preheat oven to 375°.

Mix nectarines, cherries, lemon juice and granulated sugar mixture until coated. Spoon mixture into an ungreased glass baking dish; top with cut up butter. Cover with baking foil; bake 45 minutes or until mixture is bubbly. Remove from oven.

Topping: Beat brown sugar and butter with an electric mixer until smooth. Beat in egg and vanilla. Mix oats, flour, salt and soda in another bowl; stir into creamy mixture by hand. Drop by scant ¼ cup portions over hot fruit. Return to oven. Bake uncovered until topping is browned, about 20 minutes. Refrigerate leftovers.

Makes 10 servings.

RHUBARB-CHERRY CRISP

Serve this crisp with vanilla ice cream.

1 cup uncooked quick-cooking oats
1 cup light brown sugar, packed
1 cup all-purpose flour
⅛ teaspoon salt
½ cup butter

4 cups diced fresh rhubarb
1 cup granulated sugar
1 cup water
2 tablespoons cornstarch
1 teaspoon pure vanilla extract
¼ teaspoon almond extract
1 21-ounce can cherry pie filling
½ cup chopped walnuts

Preheat oven to 350°.

Mix oats, brown sugar, flour and salt in a bowl. Cut in butter until crumbly. Press half the crumb mixture onto bottom of an ungreased 13x9-inch baking pan.

Spoon rhubarb over mixture in pan. Mix granulated sugar, water and cornstarch in a medium saucepan; stir until blended. Bring to a boil, stirring until thickened. Stir in extracts and pie filling. Spoon mixture over rhubarb; sprinkle with remaining crumb mixture. Sprinkle top with walnuts. Bake 45–55 minutes. Serve warm. Refrigerate leftovers.

Makes 8 servings.

Jams
Jellies
Preserves

FRESH CHERRY FREEZER JAM

May store in refrigerator up to 3 weeks.

2 cups stemmed, pitted and finely chopped fully ripe sweet cherries
2 tablespoons fresh lemon juice
4¼ cups granulated sugar, measured in a bowl

¾ cup water
1 (1¾-ounce) package powdered fruit pectin

Have ready clean plastic freezer containers with lids.

Mix chopped cherries, lemon juice and sugar in a bowl; let stand for 10 minutes, stirring occasionally.

Mix water and pectin in a small saucepan. Bring to a boil over high heat, stirring constantly, boiling and stirring for 1 minute. Add to cherries mixture; stir 3 minutes or until sugar is dissolved and no longer grainy.

Immediately fill containers to within ½-inch of tops. Wipe off top edges and cover with lids. Let stand at room temperature 24 hours. Jam is now ready. Freeze. Store in freezer up to 1 year. Thaw in refrigerator before using.

Makes about 5 cups.

CHERRY-RHUBARB JELLY

Keep some chilled in the refrigerator for special treats, of course.

6 cups diced fresh rhubarb
4 cups granulated sugar
1 21-ounce can cherry pie filling
1 6-ounce package cherry-flavored gelatin

Place rhubarb in a large glass bowl; stir in sugar until coated. Cover bowl and refrigerate 8 hours. Cook and stir rhubarb in a large saucepan over medium heat until tender. Stir in pie filling and dry gelatin. Bring mixture to a boil. Pour mixture into a shallow pan; cool in refrigerator. Spoon jelly into sterilized jars or freezer-safe plastic containers. Freeze.

Makes 2 pints.

TART CHERRY JELLY

Variation: Use 3 layers of damp cheesecloth instead of jelly bag.

**3½ cups prepared juice (from 3½ pounds fully ripe
   sour cherries and ½ cup water)**
1 (1¾-ounce) package fruit pectin
½ teaspoon butter or margarine, optional
4 cups granulated sugar, measured in a bowl
¼ teaspoon almond extract, optional

Bring a boiling-water canner, half-full with water, to a simmer.

Stem, pit and finely chop cherries. Place in a saucepan; add water. Bring to a boil. Reduce heat to low; cover and simmer 10 minutes, stirring occasionally. Place a jelly bag in a large bowl. Pour prepared fruit into bag; tie closed, hang and let drip into bowl until dripping stops. Press gently. Measure exactly 3½ cups, adding up to ½ cup water for exact measure; pour in an 8-quart kettle. Stir pectin into juice in kettle. Add butter to reduce foaming, if desired. Bring mixture to a full rolling boil, and boil exactly 1 minute, stirring constantly.

Quickly stir in sugar. Return to a full rolling boil on high heat, and boil exactly 1 minute, stirring constantly. Remove from heat. Skim off any foam with a metal spoon. Add extract. Immediately ladle jelly into sterilized jars, filling to within ⅛-inch of tops. Wipe jar rims and threads. Cover with two-piece lids. Screw band tightly. Place jars on elevated rack in canner. Lower rack into canner. Water must cover jars by 2 inches. Cover and bring water to a gentle boil. Process 5 minutes. Remove jars; place upright on a towel. Cool completely. Check seals by pressing finger on lids. If lids springs back the jar is not sealed, and refrigeration is required.

Makes about 5 cups.

FRESH CHERRY PRESERVES

Fresh cherry preserves and warm buttered toast...totally good.

1½ pounds fresh cherries, stemmed, pitted, very coarsely chopped
1 cup granulated sugar
1 tablespoon fresh lemon juice
¼ teaspoon almond extract

Stir cherries, sugar and lemon juice in a saucepan over medium heat until sugar is dissolved and cherries are juicy. Reduce heat to low; simmer, stirring occasionally until mixture is thickened, about 40 minutes. Stir in almond extract. Pour preserves into a glass bowl. Refrigerate; chill uncovered until cold. Store covered in refrigerator up to 2 weeks.

Makes 2 cups.

Sauces

CHERRY-APRICOT AMARETTO SAUCE

A sauce for all seasons. Try it on cheesecake or pound cake. Perfect sauce to accompany wild game, such as pheasant or duck. Use as a dipping sauce for egg rolls, etc.!

2 cups cherry juice
1 5-ounce package pitted dried cherries
½ cup diced dried apricots
2 tablespoons granulated sugar
¼ teaspoon kosher salt
1 tablespoon amaretto (almond-flavored liqueur)

Bring all ingredients except amaretto to a boil in a medium saucepan over high heat, stirring once. Reduce heat. Simmer mixture until liquid is reduced by half, about 20 minutes. Remove from heat and cool completely. Stir in amaretto. Serve. Refrigerate leftovers.

Makes about 2 cups.

CHERRY BARBECUE SAUCE

Try this tasty sauce on those grilled ribs!

1 21-ounce can cherry pie filling

2 tablespoons olive oil
½ cup chopped onion
¼ cup soy sauce
2 teaspoons spicy brown mustard
1 teaspoon ground ginger
1 teaspoon Worcestershire sauce

Puree pie filling; set aside.

Heat olive oil in a large saucepan. Add onion; stir and cook until tender. Stir in pureed cherries and remaining ingredients. Simmer uncovered, stirring occasionally, 15 minutes. Spoon mixture into a clean glass jar. Use or refrigerate up to 1 week.

Makes about 2 cups.

CHERRY ICE CREAM SAUCE

Serve plain vanilla ice cream topped with this cherry sauce...yummy.

4 cups stemmed, pitted fresh sweet cherries, halved
2½ cups granulated sugar
½ cup light corn syrup
¼ cup fresh lemon juice

1 cup water
1 (1¾-ounce) package powdered fruit pectin

Mix cherries, sugar, syrup and lemon juice in a glass bowl; let stand 30 minutes, stirring occasionally.

Bring water and fruit pectin to a boil in a medium saucepan; boil hard 1 minute. Pour mixture over cherry mixture. Stir 3 minutes. Ladle mixture into sterilized freezer food containers with tight-fitting lids. Let stand at room temperature until cool, then freeze.

Makes 6 half pints.

CHERRY SAUCE

For a brighter color, stir in 3 drops of red food coloring.

½ cup granulated sugar
2 tablespoons cornstarch
1 16-ounce can pitted red tart cherries, undrained

Mix sugar and cornstarch in a medium saucepan. Stir in cherries. Cook, stirring constantly, until mixture thickens and boils. Continue to boil and stir 1 minute. Serve with ham or pork. Refrigerate leftovers.

Makes about 2 cups.

RED WINE CHERRY SAUCE

Serve this savory sauce with fish and poultry.

1 cup stemmed and pitted fresh sweet cherries
3 tablespoons cold water
¼ cup dry red wine
3 tablespoons honey
2 tablespoons red wine vinegar
1 teaspoon fresh thyme leaves
½ teaspoon dry mustard
¼ teaspoon salt, or to taste

2 teaspoons cornstarch
1 tablespoon cold water

Mix all ingredients except cornstarch and 1 tablespoon cold water in a small saucepan. Bring to a simmer over low heat; simmer 10 minutes.

Mix cornstarch and 1 tablespoon water in a cup until smooth; stir into cherry mixture and cook until thickened. Pour sauce into a glass bowl. Serve. Refrigerate leftovers.

Makes about 1 cup.

Chutney
Relish
Salsa
Syrup

APRICOT-CHERRY CHILI CHUTNEY

Variation: 1 cup canned green chilies instead of poblano chilies.

2½ cups dried apricots, coarsely chopped
1½ cups cider vinegar
1½ cups granulated sugar
1 cup chopped roasted poblano chilies
½ cup pitted dried sweet cherries, chopped
½ cup chopped red onion
1 3-inch cinnamon stick
1½ teaspoons mustard seed
¾ teaspoon salt

Mix all ingredients in a 3-quart saucepan. Bring to a boil over high heat. Reduce heat to low. Cover and simmer mixture, stirring occasionally, until apricots are soft, about 20 minutes. Remove cover; simmer until most of the liquid evaporates, about 5 minutes. Remove from heat; cool. Discard cinnamon stick. Serve or store covered in refrigerator.

Makes about 4 cups.

FIRECRACKER SALSA

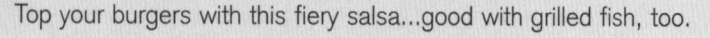

Top your burgers with this fiery salsa...good with grilled fish, too.

½ cup pitted dried tart cherries
½ cup cherry preserves
2 tablespoons red wine vinegar

½ cup chopped red onion
½ cup chopped yellow bell pepper
¼ cup chopped jalapeno pepper
1 tablespoon chopped fresh cilantro
1 teaspoon lime juice

Stir cherries, preserves and vinegar in a small microwave-safe bowl until well blended. Microwave on high until hot, about 1–1½ minutes. Let stand 5 minutes.

Stir in remaining ingredients. Cover and refrigerate at least 4 hours before serving. Store in refrigerator.

Makes about 1½ cups.

FRESH CHERRY RELISH

Nice relish for ham.

3 cups pitted tart fresh cherries
1 cup seedless raisins
1 teaspoon ground cinnamon
¼ teaspoon ground cloves
½ cup honey
½ cup vinegar
½ cup brown sugar

1 cup broken pecan or walnuts

Mix all ingredients except pecans or walnuts in a saucepan. Cook over low heat one hour. Add pecans; cook 3 minutes. Cool and place into freezer containers; freeze.

Makes about 5 cups.

FRESH CHERRY SALSA

A good condiment to serve with chicken or pork.

1 cup fresh dark sweet cherries, pitted and chopped
2 tablespoons fresh basil, chopped
1 tablespoon green pepper, finely chopped
1 teaspoon fresh lemon juice
¼ teaspoon Worcestershire sauce
¼ teaspoon freshly grated lemon peel
⅛ teaspoon salt
⅛ teaspoon Tabasco sauce

Mix all ingredients in a glass bowl. Refrigerate 1 hour before serving. Refrigerate leftovers.

Makes about ¾ cup.

MAPLE DRIED CHERRY SYRUP

Pancakes topped with this warm syrup make a breakfast to remember.

¾ cup maple syrup
½ cup brown sugar, packed
¼ cup honey
1 teaspoon fresh orange zest
½ cup fresh orange juice
3 tablespoons fresh lemon juice
1 tablespoon butter
¼ teaspoon ground cinnamon
½ cup pitted dried tart cherries

Bring all ingredients except cherries to a boil in a medium saucepan over medium heat, stirring frequently. Reduce heat; simmer 10 minutes. Stir in cherries; cook 1 minute. Pour mixture into a clean glass container. Refrigerate leftovers.

Makes 1½ cups.

Used with permission from the Cherry Marketing Institute.

Other Desserts

APRICOT-CHERRY BREAD PUDDING

Caramel sauce tops this dried fruit bread pudding.

4 cups granulated sugar, divided
2¼ cups cold water, divided
4 ounces dried apricots, thinly sliced
4 ounces dried pitted tart cherries
3 cups whipping cream, divided
2 cups whole milk
8 egg yolks
1½ loaves sliced white bread (24-ounce loaves), crust removed,
each slice cut in half

Bring 1 cup sugar, 2 cups water, apricots and cherries to a boil in a medium saucepan, stirring until sugar is dissolved. Remove from heat. Cover and steep 20 minutes. Strain fruit; reserving liquid. Cover fruit and place in refrigerator.

Mix 1 cup sugar and ¼ cup water in a saucepan. Stir over low heat until sugar is dissolved. Increase heat and boil without stirring until a deep amber color is formed, about 12 minutes. Remove from heat. Gradually whisk in 1 cup reserved liquid. Stir over low heat until caramel thickens slightly, about 6 minutes. Add 1 cup cream. Bring to a boil, then simmer until caramel thickens slightly, about 3 minutes. Remove from heat. Cool 30 minutes, whisking occasionally. Cover; refrigerate.

Preheat oven to 350°.

Bring 2 cups cream and milk to a simmer. Remove from heat. Whisk 2 cups sugar and egg yolks in a bowl until blended; gradually whisk in warm cream and milk mixture. Cool slightly. Lightly butter a 13x9x2-inch glass baking dish. Place enough bread in a layer over bottom and up sides of dish to cover; trim to fit. Sprinkle with fruit. Place remaining bread over fruit. Trim to fit, overlapping a little. Pour custard over bread. Press down. Let stand 10 minutes. Bake until set, about 55 minutes. Heat caramel sauce. Spoon over pudding when serving. Refrigerate leftovers.

Makes 8 servings.

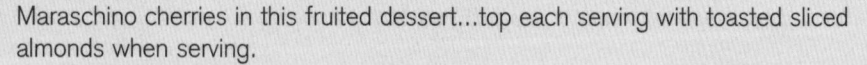

AUDREY'S AMBROSIA

Maraschino cherries in this fruited dessert...top each serving with toasted sliced almonds when serving.

1 14-ounce can sweetened condensed milk
¾ cup dairy sour cream
½ cup lime juice concentrate

½ cup maraschino cherry halves, well drained
1 20-ounce can pineapple chunks, well drained
1 11-ounce can mandarin orange segments, drained
1½ cups grape halves
1 cup flaked coconut
1 cup miniature marshmallows

Mix sweetened condensed milk, sour cream and lime juice in a large glass bowl until blended.

Stir in remaining ingredients. Refrigerate and chill well before serving. Refrigerate leftovers.

Makes 14 servings.

BLACK FOREST CREAM PUFFS

Cherry cream puffs...a delightful treat.

Cream Puffs
½ cup whole milk
½ cup cold water
½ cup butter
1 cup all-purpose flour
5 eggs

Filling
5 cups frozen unsweetened pitted tart cherries, thawed
1 cup granulated sugar
¼ cup cornstarch
¼ cup kirsch or orange juice
3 drops red food coloring
1 tablespoon pure vanilla extract

2 ounces semisweet chocolate, melted and cooled
1 cup whipping cream, whipped with 2 tablespoons powdered sugar

Preheat oven to 400°.
Cream Puffs: Mix milk, water and butter in a saucepan. Bring to a boil. Add flour all at once, stirring vigorously. Cook and stir until mixture forms a ball that does not separate. Remove from heat. Cool 5 minutes. Beat in eggs, one at a time, with a wooden spoon. Drop by heaping tablespoons onto a greased baking sheet, making 12 puffs. Bake 30 minutes or until golden. Cool on a wire rack. Split and remove any soft dough from inside.

Filling: Drain cherries; reserve juice. Stir sugar and cornstarch in a large saucepan. Stir in reserved cherry juice with enough water to measure 2 cups. Stir in kirsch and food coloring. Cook and stir over medium heat until thickened; continue cooking 2 minutes. Remove from heat. Stir in cherries and vanilla. Cover; refrigerate; chill.

To serve, spoon cherry filling inside puffs. Drizzle with chocolate. Serve with whipped cream. Refrigerate leftovers

Makes 12 servings.

121

BLACK FOREST MOUSSE

Garnish with additional whipped cream if desired.

1 1-ounce square unsweetened chocolate, melted
1 14-ounce can sweetened condensed milk
1 4-serving size package instant chocolate pudding mix
1 cup cold water
½ teaspoon almond extract
2 cups whipping cream, whipped
1 21-ounce can cherry pie filling, chilled and
   mixed with ¼ teaspoon almond extract

Mix chocolate and sweetened condensed milk in a large bowl until blended. Beat in pudding mix, water and almond extract; freeze mixture 5 minutes. Fold in whipped cream. Spoon equal portions into dessert dishes. Top with cherry pie filling mixture. Refrigerate leftovers.

Makes 10 servings.

CAKE MIX CHERRY CHEESECAKE SQUARES

Garnish each serving with thawed whipped topping.

Crust
1 18.25 package yellow cake mix
1 egg
2 tablespoons melted butter or margarine

Filling
2 8-ounce packages cream cheese, softened
½ cup granulated sugar
3 eggs
1½ cups whole milk
3 tablespoons fresh lemon juice
2 teaspoons pure vanilla extract

1 21-ounce can cherry pie filling

Preheat oven to 300°.
Grease a 13x9-inch baking pan.

Crust: Reserve 1 cup dry cake mix; set aside. Mix remaining dry cake mix, 1egg and butter in a large bowl until crumbly. Press mixture into bottom and up sides of prepared pan.

Filling: Beat cream cheese and sugar until fluffy. Add 3 eggs and reserved cake mix; beat 1 minute on medium speed. Gradually beat in milk, lemon juice and vanilla on low speed until smooth. Pour mixture into prepared crust. Bake 45–55 minutes or until center is set. Remove from oven. Cool in pan, then refrigerate. Top evenly with pie filling. Chill. Refrigerate leftovers.

Makes 12 servings.

CHERRY CHEESECAKE ICE CREAM

Variation: Use one 17-ounce can pitted dark sweet cherries, well drained and chopped, instead of maraschino cherries.

1 3-ounce package cream cheese, softened
1 14-ounce can sweetened condensed milk

2 cups half and half (light cream)
2 cups whipping cream, do not whip
1 10-ounce jar maraschino cherries, well drained, chopped
1 tablespoon pure vanilla extract
½ teaspoon almond extract

Beat cream cheese in a large bowl until fluffy. Gradually beat in sweetened condensed milk until smooth.

Add remaining ingredients to cream cheese mixture; mix well. Pour mixture into an ice cream freezer container. Freeze according to manufacturer's instructions. Freeze leftovers.

Makes about 1½ quarts.

CHERRY CLAFOUTI

Variation: Two 12-ounce bags frozen cherries, thawed and drained.

4 cups pitted fresh cherries

½ cup whipping cream
½ cup granulated sugar
2 tablespoons all-purpose flour
2 eggs
2 tablespoons butter, melted
½ teaspoon almond extract

¼ cup sliced almonds
3 tablespoons powdered sugar

Preheat oven to 375°.
Butter a 1½ quart shallow baking dish.

Place cherries into prepared baking dish.

Process cream, sugar, flour, eggs, butter and almond extract in a food processor or blender until pureed. Pour mixture over cherries.

Sprinkle with almonds. Bake uncovered 35–40 minutes or until top is golden and center is set (tent loosely with aluminum cooking foil if top browns too fast). Remove from oven; cool to room temperature. Sprinkle with powdered sugar.

Makes 8 servings.

CHERRY FLUFF

Also good as a salad when serving cold sandwiches.

1 21-ounce can cherry pie filling
1 14-ounce can sweetened condensed milk
1 20-ounce can crushed pineapple, drained
1 8-ounce container frozen nondairy whipped topping, thawed
1 cup miniature marshmallows

Mix all ingredients in a large glass bowl. Refrigerate and chill at least 2 hours before serving. Refrigerate leftovers.

Makes 12 servings.

CHERRY NUT CRÈME BRÛLÉE

A special dessert.

1 cup chopped pecans
¾ cup pitted dried tart cherries

3 cups whipping cream

8 egg yolks, lightly beaten
¼ cup granulated sugar
1 teaspoon pure vanilla extract

½ cup granulated sugar

Preheat oven to 325°.

Place equal portions of pecans and cherries into 6 custard cups; place cups into a large shallow baking pan.

Heat cream in a heavy saucepan over medium-low heat, stirring occasionally, just until bubbly but do not boil.

Mix egg yolks, ¼ cup sugar and vanilla in a large bowl. Gradually stir in warm cream. Pour mixture into custard cups. Place baking pan in oven. Add enough hot water to pan to reach halfway up sides of custard cups. Bake until a knife inserted in center comes out clean, about 35 minutes. Remove from oven. Remove custard cups form water bath; cool on a wire rack. Cover and refrigerate; chill no longer than 24 hours before serving. When serving, let stand at room temperature for 15 minutes.

Melt ½ cup sugar over medium-high heat in a heavy saucepan without stirring. When melted, reduce heat to low and cook 5 minutes, stirring occasionally. Immediately drizzle caramelized sugar over custards. Serve immediately. Refrigerate leftovers.

Makes 6 servings.

CHERRY POUND CAKE DESSERT

A good dessert to make ahead of time.

1½ cups boiling water
1 package (8-serving size) cherry flavor gelatin
1½ cups cold water
1 21-ounce can cherry pie filling

1 12-ounce purchased pound cake, cut into 10 slices
2 cups thawed nondairy whipped topping

Stir boiling water into dry gelatin in a large bowl until completely dissolved. Stir in cold water and cherry pie filling. Refrigerate until slightly thickened, about 1¼ hours.

Line bottom of a 13x9x2-inch glass baking dish with cake slices. Spoon gelatin mixture over cake. Refrigerate 2 hours or until firm. Spread with whipped topping just before serving. Refrigerate leftovers.

Makes 16 servings.

CHERRY TRIFLE

Use purchased pound cake to make this simple dessert.

1 package (4 serving size) instant vanilla pudding and pie filling
2 cups cold whole milk

1 10-ounce pound cake
¼ cup fresh orange juice
1 21-ounce can cherry pie filling
1½ cups frozen nondairy whipped topping, thawed, divided
½ cup sliced almonds, lightly toasted

Prepare pudding with milk as directed on package; let stand 5 minutes.

Cut pound cake into ¼-inch slices. Brush slices with orange juice. Line bottom and sides of a 2-quart serving bowl with a third of the cake slices. Layer half of the pudding, a third of the pie filling, ½ cup of whipped topping and a third of the cake slices. Repeat layers. Spread remaining whipped topping over all. Spread remaining pie filling into center, leaving a 1-inch border. Sprinkle almonds around edge. Refrigerate 30 minutes before serving. Refrigerate leftovers.

Makes 8 servings.

CHERRY YUM YUM

This yummy dessert comes from South Carolina...thanks Margie.

2 envelopes whipped topping mix

2 8-ounce package cream cheese, softened
¾ cup granulated sugar
1 teaspoon pure vanilla extract

8 tablespoons margarine, melted
1 13-ounce box graham cracker crumbs
2 21-ounce cans cherry pie filling

Mix dry whipped topping following instructions on box.

Beat cream cheese, sugar and vanilla in a bowl; add to whipped topping mixture and mix well.

Mix melted margarine with graham crack crumbs in a bowl; set aside.

In a large glass-serving bowl, form layers starting with graham cracker crumbs, then cherries and then the whipped topping. Repeat layers until all ingredients are used. Chill. Store in refrigerator.

Makes 12 servings.

CHOCOLATE CHERRY SHORTCAKE

Kirsch whipping cream tops these shortcakes.

Shortcake
- **2 cups all-purpose flour**
- **¼ cup granulated sugar**
- **1 tablespoon baking powder**
- **½ teaspoon salt**
- **½ cup cold butter, cut into small pieces**
- **3 ounces semisweet chocolate, coarsely grated**
- **1 large egg beaten in a small bowl with ½ cup whole milk**

Cherries
- **1½ pounds fresh Bing cherries, stemmed, pitted, halved**
- **¼ cup granulated sugar**
- **1 tablespoon kirsch (cherry brandy)**
- **⅓ cup cherry jam**

Topping
- **1½ cups whipping cream, whipped in a bowl to stiff peaks with 2 tablespoons granulated sugar and 1 tablespoon kirsch**

Preheat oven to 400°.
Line a large baking sheet with parchment paper.

Shortcake: Mix flour, sugar, baking powder and salt. Cut in butter until mixture resembles coarse meal. Stir in chocolate. Gradually add egg mixture, tossing with a fork until dough is moistened. Knead 5 times on a floured surface; form into an 8-inch log. Cut crosswise into 8 biscuits; shape each into 2½x¾-inch biscuits. Place on baking sheet. Bake about 15 minutes. Cool completely.

Cherries: Mix cherries, sugar and kirsch in a glass bowl; let stand 3 hours. Strain juice into a heavy saucepan. Stir in jam. Cook, stirring often, over medium heat until thick syrup is formed. Mix syrup into cherries.

Cut biscuits in half horizontally. Place bottom in dessert bowls; top each with cherry mixture and whipped cream. Cover with tops. Refrigerate leftovers.

Makes 8 servings.

CHOCOLATE CHERRY TRUFFLES

A perfect after-dinner treat.

12 1-ounce squares semisweet chocolate
3 1-ounce squares unsweetened chocolate
1 14-ounce can sweetened condensed milk
¼ teaspoon salt

2 tablespoons cherry-flavored liqueur, optional
¼ cup chopped nuts
½ cup drained and chopped maraschino cherries

2 6-ounce packages premium white chocolate baking bars
2 teaspoons vegetable oil
assorted colored sprinkles

Heat semisweet and unsweetened chocolate, sweetened condensed milk and salt in a saucepan over medium heat, stirring constantly until chocolate is melted, about 7 minutes. Remove from heat.

Stir in liqueur, nuts and cherries. Cover surface directly with waxed paper; refrigerate until cold, about 2 hours.

Scoop out a tablespoonful of cold mixture. Roll between clean hands to form a smooth ball. Place on baking sheet lined with waxed paper. Repeat.

Melt white chocolate with oil in a small saucepan over low heat, stirring constantly. Remove from heat and let stand until cool to touch, about 1 minute. Using 2 forks, dip balls into white chocolate. Place on waxed paper to dry. Decorate as desired with sprinkles. Store in refrigerator.

Makes 3½ dozen.

CHOCOLATE MOUSSE WITH CHERRY SAUCE

White chocolate is used in this elegant dessert.

2 egg yolks, beaten
½ cup whole milk
3 tablespoons granulated sugar
1 teaspoon cornstarch

3 1-ounce squares white baking chocolate, grated
½ teaspoon pure vanilla extract

1½ cups whipping cream

Sauce
½ cup granulated sugar
2 tablespoons cornstarch
½ cup water
2 cups pitted fresh red cherries
½ teaspoon pure vanilla extract
1 tablespoon orange juice

Mix eggs, milk, 3 tablespoons sugar and 1 teaspoon cornstarch in a small saucepan. Cook and stir over medium heat until bubbly and slightly thickened. Remove from heat. Stir in chocolate until melted. Stir in vanilla. Cool to room temperature.

Whip cream to soft peaks; gently fold into cooled chocolate mixture. Spoon into a 2-quart baking dish. Refrigerate until set, about 4 hours.

Sauce: Mix sugar and cornstarch in a saucepan. Stir in water until smooth. Stir in cherries. Cook and stir over medium heat until bubbly and thickened; continue stirring and cooking another 2 minutes. Remove from heat. Stir in vanilla and orange juice. Cool slightly before serving.

Spoon chocolate mixture into dessert dishes. Top with warm cherry sauce. Refrigerate leftovers.

Makes 6 servings.

CREAM CHEESE CHERRY DESSERT

Cherry pie filling and cream cheese...a good make-ahead dessert.

1¼ cups graham cracker crumbs
⅓ cup margarine or butter, melted

1 8-ounce package cream cheese, softened
½ cup powdered sugar
1 tablespoon whole milk
¼ teaspoon pure almond extract
½ cup chopped pecans

¼ cup powdered sugar
1 cup whipping cream
1 21-ounce can cherry pie filling
¼ teaspoon pure almond extract

Mix graham cracker crumbs and margarine in a bowl; press mixture onto bottom of a 9x9-inch baking dish.

Mix cream cheese, ½ cup sugar, milk and ¼ teaspoon almond extract in a bowl until well blended. Spread evenly over crust. Sprinkle with pecans.

Gradually add ¼ cup sugar to whipping cream in a bowl, beating until stiff peaks form. Spread mixture over pecans. Mix pie filling and ¼ teaspoon almond extract; spread over whipped cream layer. Refrigerate and chill several hours before serving. Refrigerate leftovers.

Makes 8 servings.

FRESH CHERRIES JUBILEE

A classic dessert.

½ **cup granulated sugar**
1 **tablespoon cornstarch**
¼ **cup water**
¼ **cup fresh orange juice**
3 **cups pitted fresh sweet cherries**
½ **teaspoon freshly grated orange peel**

¼ **cup brandy, optional**
1 **quart vanilla ice cream**

Mix sugar and cornstarch in a heavy sauce pan. Stir in water and orange juice until blended. Cook, stirring constantly, until thickened. Add cherries and orange peel; bring to a boil. Reduce heat and simmer 10 minutes. Remove from heat.

Gently heat brandy in a small saucepan. Pour over cherry mixture. Flame, if desired. Stir gently and ladle over ice cream.

Makes 8 servings.

FRESH CHERRY-BERRY ICE CREAM

Call the kids!

2 envelopes unflavored gelatin
1½ cups granulated sugar
½ cup water
1 10-ounce package frozen sliced strawberries

4 cups light cream or half & half
2 cups whipping cream
2 teaspoons pure vanilla extract
2 cups dark sweet cherries, chopped

Mix gelatin and sugar in a small saucepan. Stir in water and strawberries. Cook over medium heat, stirring constantly, until mixture just comes to a boil. Remove from heat; cool to room temperature.

Mix half & half, whipping cream, vanilla, strawberry mixture and cherries in a 3-quart (or larger) ice cream maker. Freeze according to manufacturer's directions, or place in freezer containers and freeze at least 4 hours. Freeze leftovers.

Makes 3 quarts.

FRESH CHERRY CHOCOLATE ICE CREAM

Adult treat.

2 cups pitted fresh sweet cherries
2 tablespoons cherry brandy

1 quart vanilla ice cream, softened
4 ounces bittersweet or semisweet chocolate, coarsely chopped

Process cherries in food processor until almost smooth but leaving some small pieces intact. Place in a bowl. Stir in brandy. Let stand at room temperature 1 hour.

Place ice cream in a large bowl. Stir in cherry mixture. Stir in chocolate. Cover and freeze until firm, about 4 hours. Freeze leftovers.

Makes 1 quart.

FRESH CHERRY CLAFOUTIS

A special fresh cherry dessert.

4 eggs
1 cup granulated sugar, divided
1 vanilla bean split in half
1 tablespoon cherry brandy
1 cup all-purpose flour
1½ cups whole milk

1 pound pitted fresh cherries
powdered sugar

Preheat oven to 350°.
Grease an oval 13-inch long baking dish.

Whisk eggs and ½ cup granulated sugar in a bowl. Scrape vanilla bean; add pulp to mixture. Stir in brandy and flour. Whisk in milk to form smooth batter.

Mix cherries and remaining granulated sugar in a bowl. Spoon into prepared baking dish. Pour batter over cherries.

Bake 40–45 minutes. Remove from oven; cool slightly before serving. Serve warm. Garnish with powdered sugar. Refrigerate leftovers.

Makes 6 servings.

FRESH CHERRY SLUMP

Fresh cherries and prunes in this dessert…serve warm.

1 cup pitted fresh sweet cherries
2 cups sliced pitted prunes
½ cup granulated sugar
¼ cup cold water

Topping
¾ cup all-purpose flour
¼ cup granulated sugar
1 teaspoon baking powder
1 teaspoon ground cinnamon
⅛ teaspoon salt
3 tablespoons butter
⅓ cup milk

Mix cherries, prunes, ½ cup sugar and ¼ cup water in a 3-quart saucepan. Bring to a boil, then reduce heat.

Topping: Mix flour, ¼ cup sugar, baking powder, cinnamon and salt in a bowl. Cut in butter until coarse crumbs form. Stir in milk just to moisten.

Spoon dough in 6 mounds on top of hot fruit mixture. Cover and simmer about 15 minutes or until a wooden pick inserted in topping comes out clean. Refrigerate leftovers.

Makes 6 servings.

FRIED FRESH CHERRIES

Appetizer or dessert.

1 pound fresh ripe red fresh cherries
1 cup all-purpose flour
¼ cup granulated sugar
⅓ cup whole milk
⅓ cup dry white wine
3 eggs

corn oil for frying
powdered sugar
ground cinnamon

Wash cherries and wipe dry. Leave stems on. Tie stems with thread to form clusters of 4 cherries each.

Heat oil in a deep heavy kettle to 375° on a frying thermometer.

Mix flour, sugar, milk, wine and eggs in a bowl to form a smooth batter. Dip each cluster of cherries into batter, coating well. Fry clusters in hot oil until golden. Remove with a slotted spoon; drain on paper towels. Sprinkle with powdered sugar and cinnamon. Serve immediately.

Makes 6 servings.

FROZEN CHERRIES CREAM DESSERT

A creamy frozen cherry dessert.

2 cups chocolate cookie crumbs
⅓ cup granulated sugar
⅓ cup butter or margarine, melted

2 cups heavy cream
1 14-ounce can sweetened condensed milk
1 teaspoon pure vanilla extract

1 21-ounce can cherry pie filling
½ cup slivered almonds, coarsely chopped
½ cup miniature semisweet chocolate chips

Mix cookie crumbs, sugar and butter in a bowl; press mixture into bottom of a 13x9x2-inch baking dish.

Mix heavy cream, sweetened condensed milk and vanilla extract in a large bowl until blended. Cover and refrigerate 30 minutes. Beat mixture with an electric mixer on medium speed until soft peaks form, about 3–4 minutes. Do not over beat.

Gently fold in cherry pie filling, almonds and chocolate chips. Spoon mixture over crumb crust. Cover and freeze at least 6 hours. When serving, uncover and let stand 10 minutes at room temperature. Cut into squares. Freeze leftovers.

Makes 15 servings.

ICE CREAM PUFFS WITH PRALINE CHERRY SAUCE

Warm sauce tops these ice cream filled puffs.

Puffs
1 cup cold water
½ cup butter
¼ teaspoon salt
1 cup all-purpose flour
4 eggs

1 quart vanilla ice cream

Sauce
½ cup brown sugar, packed
½ cup corn syrup
¼ cup butter
½ cup chopped pecans
⅓ cup well drained chopped maraschino cherries
1 teaspoon pure vanilla extract

Preheat oven to 400°.

Puffs: Mix water, butter and salt to in a 2-quart saucepan; cook until mixture comes to a full boil, about 5 minutes. Add flour; stir until mixture leaves sides of pan and forms a ball, about 1 minute. Remove from heat; cool 3 minutes. Beat in eggs one at a time until well blended. Drop ¼ cup batter onto greased baking sheet to form 12 puffs. Bake until puffed and light brown, about 30–35 minutes. Cool on a wire rack.

Sauce: Cook and stir sugar, syrup and butter in a saucepan over medium heat until mixtures comes to a full boil. Remove from heat. Stir in pecans, cherries and vanilla.

To serve, slice off top of cream puffs; remove and discard excess dough, if any. Fill each puff with ⅓ cup vanilla ice cream; replace top. Top with warm sauce as desired. Refrigerate leftovers.

Makes 12 servings.

LOLA'S CHERRY-BERRY ON A CLOUD

Lola lives in Minneapolis, Minnesota, and shares this delicious dessert.

6 egg whites
½ teaspoon cream of tartar
¼ teaspoon salt
1¾ cups granulated sugar

Filling
2 3-ounce packages cream cheese
1 cup granulated sugar
1 teaspoon pure vanilla extract
2 cup thawed whipped topping
2 cups miniature marshmallows

Topping
1 21-ounce can cherry pie filling
1 teaspoon fresh lemon juice
2 cups sliced strawberries

Preheat oven to 275°.
Grease a 13x9-inch baking pan.

Beat egg whites, cream of tartar and salt with an electric mixer in a large bowl until frothy. Gradually beat in 1¾ cups sugar until stiff, about 15 minutes. Spread mixture into prepared pan. Bake for 1 hour. Turn oven off and leave in oven until cool.

Filling: Beat cream cheese, sugar and vanilla in a large bowl with an electric mixer until creamy. Fold in whipped topping and marshmallows. Spread mixture over baked meringue and immediately refrigerate. Refrigerate 12 hours before topping with fruit.

Topping: Mix pie filling, lemon juice and strawberries in a bowl; chill. Spoon topping mixture over filling when serving. Store in refrigerator.

Makes 12 servings.

MOOSE'S CHERRY SORBET

A cool summer dessert...perfect for those Louisiana summers!

1 21-ounce can cherry pie filling
¾ cup frozen cherry juice blend concentrate, thawed, undiluted
½ teaspoon freshly grated lemon peel
2 tablespoons fresh lemon juice
½ teaspoon pure almond extract, optional

toasted slivered almonds
mini semisweet chocolate chips

Process first 5 ingredients in a blender or food processor until smooth, about 20 seconds. Pour into a 9x9x2-inch pan or glass baking dish. Cover with aluminum foil and freeze about 8 hours. Mixture will be slushy but will not freeze firm.

When serving, remove sorbet from freezer and stir with a fork. Spoon into dessert bowls. Top with almonds and chocolate chips as desired. Store leftovers in the freezer.

Makes 6 servings.

MR. BROWN'S ANGEL CHERRY CREAM DESSERT

Angel food and cherries...just like Mr. Brown, total delight.

1 10-ounce prepared round angel food cake, frozen for easy slicing

1 14-ounce can sweetened condensed milk
1 cup cold water
1 teaspoon pure vanilla extract
1 4-serving size package instant vanilla pudding mix

2 cups whipping cream, whipped with 2 tablespoons granulated
sugar and ½ teaspoon pure vanilla extract
2 21-ounce cans cherry pie filling

Cut frozen cake into ¼-inch slices and arrange half the slices on bottom of a 13x9-inch glass baking dish.

Beat sweetened condensed milk, water and 1 teaspoon vanilla extract in a large bowl with an electric mixer until blended. Beat in pudding mix until well mixed. Chill 5 minutes.

Fold in whipped cream. Spread half the cream mixture over cake slices. Top evenly with one can pie filling. Top with remaining cake slices, then top with remaining cream mixture and remaining pie filling. Chill 4 hours or until set. Cut into squares to serve. Refrigerate leftovers.

Makes 12 servings.

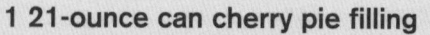

NELAN'S CHERRY DESSERT

A quick and delicious chiffon dessert.

1 21-ounce can cherry pie filling
1 15-ounce can pineapple chunks in juice or
   crushed pineapple in juice, well drained and chilled
1 14-ounce can sweetened condensed milk (not evaporated milk)
1 8-ounce container frozen nondairy whipped topping, thawed
1 cup miniature marshmallows

toasted slivered almonds

Mix all ingredients except almonds in a large glass-serving bowl. Refrigerate and chill at least 30 minutes before serving.

Top each serving with slivered almonds as desired. Refrigerate leftovers.

Makes 8 servings.

PINEAPPLE-CHERRY TRIFLE

*A 6-quart clear glass serving bowl may be used instead of a trifle dish.

1 18.25-ounce package moist yellow cake mix

1 4-serving size package vanilla instant pudding mix

1 15-ounce can crushed pineapple, drained
1 21-ounce can cherry pie filling
3½ cups flaked coconut (12-ounce package)
2 cups chopped pecans
2 8-ounce containers frozen nondairy whipped topping, thawed

Preheat oven to 350°.
Grease and flour two 9-inch round cake baking pans.

Prepare, bake and cool cake following package directions.

Prepare pudding following package directions; refrigerate until used.

Crumble one baked cake layer in a 6-quart *trifle dish.
Layer half each of pudding, pineapple, cherry pie filling, coconut, pecans and whipped topping. Repeat layers, beginning with crumbling second cake layer. Refrigerate until ready to serve. Refrigerate leftovers.

Makes 24 servings.

RED WINE POACHED SWEET CHERRIES

Good served cold too.

2¼ cups red wine
1 cup granulated sugar
1 strip fresh orange zest (1x3 inches)
2 pounds sweet cherries halved and pitted

1 cup mascarpone cheese
2½ tablespoons honey

Bring wine, sugar and orange strip to a simmer in a medium stainless-steel saucepan over medium high heat. Add cherries and bring back to a simmer. Reduce heat; simmer partially covered until cherries are just tender, about 5 minutes. Pour mixture into a glass bowl; discard orange.

Mix the cheese and honey in a small bowl until blended.

Serve warm cherries and syrup in bowls or stemmed glasses, topped with a large dollop of cheese mixture. Refrigerate leftovers.

Makes 4 servings.

RICE PUDDING WITH CHERRY SAUCE

Rice pudding topped with hot cherry sauce.

4¾ cups whole milk
5 tablespoons granulated sugar
¾ cup short grain rice
1 vanilla bean, split lengthwise
½ cup sliced almonds, toasted

1 cup whipping cream
2 tablespoons granulated sugar

1 16-ounce package frozen pitted cherries, thawed
1 lemon cut into 4 pieces
¾ cup granulated sugar
1 tablespoon cornstarch mixed in a cup with 1 tablespoon water

---

Mix milk, 5 tablespoons sugar and rice in a heavy medium saucepan. Scrape in seeds from vanilla bean and add to saucepan along with bean. Bring to a boil. Reduce heat to medium; simmer until rice is tender and mixture is thick, stirring often, about 35 minutes. Discard vanilla bean. Stir in almonds. Pour into a 13x9x2-inch baking pan. Cool completely.

Beat whipping cream and 2 tablespoons sugar with an electric mixer to medium peaks. Fold into cool rice pudding mixture. Cover; refrigerate until cold.

Cook cherries, lemon and ¾ cup sugar in a heavy medium saucepan over medium heat until cherries are tender, about 5 minutes. Stir in cornstarch mixture; bring to a boil, stirring constantly. Discard lemon. Spoon pudding into dessert bowls; top with hot cherry sauce. Refrigerate leftovers.

Makes 6 servings.

RUTH'S CHOCOLATE CHERRY DESSERT

Simple to prepare...and delicious.

1 (4-serving size) box chocolate instant pudding and pie filling mix
2 cups cold whole milk
1 21-ounce can cherry pie filling
2 cups frozen nondairy whipped topping, thawed
toasted slivered almonds, optional

Beat dry pudding mix and milk in a bowl with an electric mixer on low speed about 2 minutes or until well blended. Let pudding thicken slightly. Stir in cherry pie filling. Fold in thawed whipped topping; spoon into dessert dishes. Refrigerate and chill until ready to serve. Sprinkle each serving with toasted almonds, if desired. Refrigerate leftovers.

Makes 8 servings.

ULTIMATE BOWL OF CHERRIES

* Choose white chocolate with cocoa butter listed in ingredients.

1¼ pounds *white chocolate, coarsely chopped
2½ cups heavy cream
2 tablespoons pure vanilla extract

1 pound fresh stemmed and pitted cherries
1½ pound frozen mixed berries

Mix chocolate, heavy cream and vanilla in a heat-proof bowl. Place it over a pan of simmering water, over medium heat, until the chocolate melts.

Place equal portions of cherries and frozen berries in individual dessert bowls; let stand 5 minutes. Ladle warm chocolate sauce over cherries and berries; serve at once. Refrigerate leftovers.

Makes 8 servings.

UPSIDE-DOWN CHERRY PUDDING

When baked the cherries and sauce will be on the bottom of the pan.
This recipe comes from Houston, Texas...thanks cousin Jane.

1½ cups all-purpose flour
1½ teaspoons baking powder
¼ teaspoon salt

½ cup butter
1 cup granulated sugar
1 egg
1 teaspoon pure vanilla extract
1 cup whole milk

Sauce
1 cup granulated sugar
1 16-ounce can pitted sour red
  cherries, undrained
½ cup boiling water

Preheat oven to 350°.
Butter a 9x9-inch baking pan.

Sift flour with baking powder and salt twice in a medium bowl; set aside.

Beat butter and 1 cup sugar in a large bowl until light and fluffy. Beat in egg and
vanilla extract. Add flour mixture alternately with milk, beginning and ending with
flour, beating well after each addition. Pour batter into prepared pan.

Sauce: Stir all sauce ingredients in a small saucepan over medium heat until sugar
is dissolved. Pour mixture over batter. Bake 35–45 minutes or until pudding begins
to pull away from sides and top is golden.

Serve warm or cool with whipped cream, if desired. Refrigerate leftovers.

Makes 8 servings.

WHITE CHOCOLATE BREAD PUDDING

* For best flavor, use white chocolate with cocoa butter listed in the ingredients.

1 pound *white chocolate, coarsely chopped

1 quart light cream
½ cup granulated sugar
6 eggs, slightly beaten
2 teaspoons pure vanilla extract
½ teaspoon ground cinnamon

1 16-ounce loaf day-old Italian bread cut into ¾-inch cubes
1 cup pitted dried tart cherries

Preheat oven to 350°.
Spray a 13x9x2-inch baking pan with nonstick cooking spray.

Melt chocolate in a large heavy saucepan over medium heat, stirring often.

Mix cream and sugar in a saucepan, over medium heat, stirring occasionally until sugar is dissolved and mixture is hot but not boiling. Pour mixture over melted chocolate. Cover and let stand 5 minutes, then stir until well blended. Stir in eggs, vanilla extract and cinnamon.

Place half of bread cubes into prepare pan. Layer with half the cherries. Then layer with half the chocolate mixture. Repeat layers. Press down gently on top of bread cubes. Cover with aluminum foil. Bake 50–60 minutes or until a knife inserted in center comes out clean. Cool slightly before serving. Top with sweetened whipped cream. Refrigerate leftovers.

Makes 12 servings.

Meals
Paired with
Cherries

ALMOND CHERRY STUFFED CHICKEN BREASTS

Serve with a crisp salad and rice pilaf.

4 boneless skinless chicken breasts

6 ounces goat cheese
¼ cup coarsely chopped pitted dried cherries
½ cup coarsely chopped almonds, divided
½ teaspoon lemon zest
¼ teaspoon kosher salt
⅛ teaspoon freshly ground pepper
½ cup coarse bread crumbs
1 large egg, lightly beaten in a bowl

1½ tablespoons olive oil

Flatten chicken between waxed paper with the flat side of a meat mallet or a rolling pin; set aside.

Mix cheese, cherries, ¼ cup almonds and lemon zest in a bowl. Place one fourth of the mixture at one end of each chicken breast and roll tucking in ends. Sprinkle with salt and pepper. Mix remaining almonds and bread crumbs on a plate. Dip each breast in egg, then roll all sides in bread crumb mixture. Place in freezer on a plate for one hour.

Preheat oven to 375°.
Heat oil in a large ovenproof skillet over medium-high heat. Cook chicken until golden (6-8 minutes). Place skillet in oven and finish cooking until chicken is no longer pink, juices run clear and temperature reaches 170° (about 20 minutes). Serve hot. Refrigerate leftovers.

Makes 20 servings.

BANANA SPLIT FRENCH TOAST

Sunday breakfast French toast... kids will love this special treat.

1 8-ounce package cream cheese, softened
¼ cup powdered sugar
1 10-ounce jar maraschino cherries

3 eggs
⅔ cup whole milk
1 16-ounce loaf French bread

2 tablespoons butter, or as needed

4 large ripe bananas
sweetened whipped cream
chocolate-flavored syrup
toasted chopped pecans

Beat cream cheese and powdered sugar in a medium bowl until creamy. Drain cherries; reserve 8, cut in half for garnish. Chop remaining cherries; stir into cheese mixture; set aside.

Blend eggs and milk in a shallow bowl; set aside.

Cut ends off bread; discard. Slice remaining loaf into 16 ½-inch slices. Dip bread into egg mixture, coating both sides. Melt 1 tablespoon butter in a large nonstick skillet over medium heat. Cook bread slices in batches, adding more butter as needed. Cook until golden, turning once.

Slice bananas in half lengthwise, then in half crosswise. Spread 2 tablespoons cream cheese mixture onto each slice of cooked French toast; top with banana quarter. Top with whipped cream, reserved cherry halves, chocolate syrup and pecans.

Makes 8 servings.

Used with permission from the Cherry Marketing Institute.

BEEF, BEANS AND CHERRY BAKE

Serve this hot dish with green salad and crusty rolls.

1 pound ground beef

2 16-ounce cans pork and beans in tomato sauce
1 15-ounce can kidney beans, drained
1 cup ketchup
1 envelope dry onion soup mix (1⅜-ounce)
½ cup cold water
2 tablespoons prepared yellow mustard
2 teaspoons cider vinegar
2 cups frozen unsweetened tart pitted cherries

Preheat oven to 400°.

Stir and cook ground beef in a large saucepan until browned. Drain fat.

Add remaining ingredients; stir well. Spoon mixture into a 2½-quart baking dish.
Bake uncovered about 30 minutes or until bubbly and very hot. Refrigerate leftovers.

Makes 8 servings.

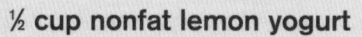

CHERRY CHICKEN WRAPS

Serve with your favorite beverage.

½ cup nonfat lemon yogurt
1 tablespoon coarse-grain honey mustard
1 teaspoon Worcestershire sauce
¾ teaspoon curry powder
¼ teaspoon salt
¼ teaspoon coarsely ground black pepper

1½ cups finely chopped cooked chicken (8-ounces)
1 cup pitted dried tart cherries
½ cup finely chopped seeded cucumber
⅓ cup shredded carrot
¼ cup sliced green onions
4 8-inch tomato-flavored flour tortillas or whole wheat flour tortillas,
   heated following package directions.

Mix yogurt, mustard, Worcestershire sauce, curry powder, salt and pepper in a medium bowl until blended.

Stir in chicken, cherries, cucumber, carrot and green onions. Spoon ¾ cup mixture just below center of each tortilla. Fold in sides, just covering edges of mixture. Roll up from one side, jelly-roll style. Serve seam side down. Refrigerate leftovers.

Makes 4 servings.

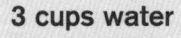

CHERRY PECAN OATMEAL

Serve with milk or cream.

3 cups water
3 cups milk
2 cups rolled oats
½ cup dried cherries, coarsely chopped
½ teaspoon salt

5 tablespoons brown sugar, divided
1 tablespoon butter
¼ teaspoon ground cinnamon
¼ teaspoon pure vanilla extract
2 tablespoons toasted chopped pecans

Bring first 5 ingredients to a boil in a saucepan. Reduce heat and simmer, stirring occasionally, 20 minutes or until thickened. Remove from heat. Stir in 4 tablespoons brown sugar, butter, cinnamon and vanilla. Spoon 1 cup oats into each of 6 bowls. Sprinkle each evenly with pecans and remaining brown sugar. Serve immediately. Refrigerate leftovers.

Makes 6 servings.

CHICKEN CHERRY SALAD SANDWICH

Tart cherries in this chicken salad. Serve with potato chips.

2 cups cubed cooked chicken
½ cup pitted dried tart cherries
3 green onions, thinly sliced

½ cup mayonnaise
¼ cup plain yogurt
1 tablespoon fresh lemon juice
salt to taste
freshly ground black pepper to taste

lettuce leaves
croissants, buttered

Mix chicken, cherries and onions in a glass bowl.

Mix mayonnaise, yogurt, lemon juice, salt and pepper in a bowl until blended; stir into chicken mixture. Cover and refrigerate until chilled, about 1 hour. Spoon mixture on half of each croissant, top with lettuce. Top with remaining half of croissant. Refrigerate leftovers.

Makes 4 servings.

PORK CHERRY WRAPS

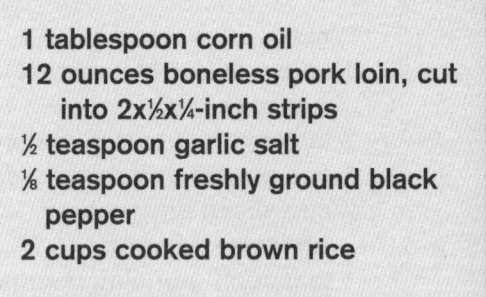

Variation: Use chicken strips instead of pork; cooked the same way.

3 cups pitted fresh sweet cherries, divided
2 tablespoons chopped fresh basil
2 tablespoons finely chopped Anaheim pepper
2 teaspoons grated fresh ginger root, divided
¼ teaspoon salt

1 tablespoon corn oil
12 ounces boneless pork loin, cut into 2x½x¼-inch strips
½ teaspoon garlic salt
⅛ teaspoon freshly ground black pepper
2 cups cooked brown rice

8 10-inch flour tortillas
2 cups shredded romaine lettuce

Chop 2 cups cherries in a food processor; spoon in a medium bowl. Stir in basil, Anaheim pepper, ginger and salt; set aside.

Heat corn oil in a saucepan over medium heat. Add pork; season with garlic and black pepper. Stir and cook until done. Stir in 1 cup cherries. Fold in rice.

Preheat oven to 350°.
Wrap tortillas in heavy cooking foil; place in oven and heat until warm, about 10 minutes. Remove from oven. Spoon ¼ cup each: pork mixture, lettuce and chopped cherry mixture, on one half of each warm tortilla. Fold sides and roll into a bundle. Serve. Refrigerate leftovers.

Makes 4 servings.

SAUCY CHERRY-APPLE PUFF PANCAKE

Serve this breakfast or brunch treat with steaming mugs of fresh coffee.

Pancake
- 1½ cups buttermilk complete pancake mix
- 2 tablespoons butter, melted
- 1 cup peeled and thinly sliced apples
- ⅓ cup sliced almonds or chopped pecans
- 1 teaspoon granulated sugar mixed with ¼ teaspoon ground cinnamon
- 3 tablespoons maple syrup

Cherry Sauce
- 1 21-ounce can light cherry pie filling
- 2 tablespoons butter
- ¼ cup brown sugar
- ⅛ cup light corn syrup
- 1 teaspoon almond extract

Preheat oven to 400°.
Spray a 10-inch deep-dish pie plate with butter cooking spray.

Pancake: Prepare pancake mix according to package directions; set aside.

Add melted butter to pie plate. Arrange apple slices on top of butter. Sprinkle with almonds and sugar-cinnamon mixture. Drizzle with syrup. Carefully pour pancake batter on top. Bake 25 minutes or until top springs back when touched. Remove from oven. Loosen edges, then invert onto a serving plate. Cut into wedges. Serve immediately with warm cherry sauce.

Cherry Sauce: Bring all ingredients to a boil in a medium saucepan over medium heat. Reduce heat; cook 5 minutes, stirring occasionally. Serve warm. Refrigerate leftovers.

Makes 8 servings.

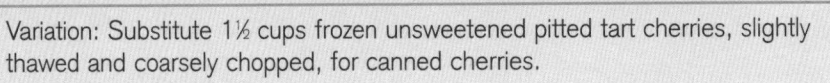

SAUSAGE CHERRY BRUNCH PIE

Variation: Substitute 1½ cups frozen unsweetened pitted tart cherries, slightly thawed and coarsely chopped, for canned cherries.

½ pound bulk pork sausage
1 16-ounce can pitted tart cherries, drained, coarsely chopped
1 cup shredded sharp Cheddar cheese (about 4 ounces)

1 cup all-purpose buttermilk baking mix
1 teaspoon dried basil
½ teaspoon salt
⅛ teaspoon ground black pepper
4 eggs, slightly beaten
1½ cups whole milk

Preheat oven to 400°.

Stir and cook sausage in a skillet over medium heat until brown. Remove from heat; drain fat. Stir in cherries. Spoon mixture into a 10-inch deep-dish pie baking plate. Top with cheese.

Mix baking mix, basil, salt and pepper in a medium bowl until blended. Add eggs and milk; beat until smooth. Pour over cheese.

Bake 35–40 minutes or until a knife inserted in center comes out clean. Remove from oven. Cool 5 minutes. Cut into wedges. Serve immediately. Refrigerate leftovers.

Makes 6 servings.

TURKEY CHERRY ROLL

Good sliced cold too. Serve with cherry sauce.

1 boneless skinless turkey
breast half

1 tablespoon corn oil
¼ cup chopped celery
¼ cup chopped water chestnuts
2 tablespoons chopped onion

1 cup coarsely chopped pitted fresh
sweet cherries
1 cup coarse dried bread crumbs
2 teaspoons fresh chopped sage
1 teaspoon fresh chopped rosemary
½ teaspoon salt
¼ teaspoon freshly ground black pepper
1 teaspoon corn oil
ground paprika

Preheat oven to 325°.

Cut breast horizontally toward thick edge to within ¾ inch of edge. Do not cut through. Pound between two sheets of cooking plastic wrap with a meat mallet to form a rectangle shape ½-inch thick.

Heat 1 tablespoon corn oil in a large saucepan. Stir and cook celery, water chestnuts and onion over medium heat until just tender. Add cherries, bread crumbs, sage, rosemary, salt and pepper. Mix well. Remove plastic from turkey. Spread with cooked mixture within 1 inch along long edge. Roll tightly; secure with skewers. Brush with 1 teaspoon corn oil. Sprinkle with paprika over all. Place on a rack in a baking pan. Bake 50–60 minutes or to internal temperature of 170°. Remove from oven; let stand a few minutes before slicing. Serve hot. Refrigerate leftovers.

Makes 8 servings.

Pies
Pastries

BLACK FOREST PIE

Black Forest treat...yummy.

1 9-inch baked pastry shell

4 1-ounce squares unsweetened baking chocolate
1 14-ounce can sweetened condensed milk
1 teaspoon almond extract
1½ cups whipping cream, whipped

1 21-ounce can cherry pie filling, chilled
toasted sliced almonds

Stir chocolate and sweetened condensed milk in a heavy saucepan over low heat until chocolate is melted. Remove from heat. Stir in almond extract. Pour mixture into a large bowl; refrigerate and chill well. Beat until smooth. Fold in whipped cream.

Pour mixture into baked pastry shell. Refrigerate and chill 4 hours or until set. Top each serving with cherry pie filling. Garnish with almonds. Refrigerate leftovers.

Makes 8 servings.

BLUEBERRY-CHERRY PIE

For quick preparation, use a 15-ounce package refrigerated pie crusts prepared as directed on package for a 9-inch pie pan.

Crust
Pastry for a double crust 9-inch pie.

Filling
½ cup granulated sugar
2 tablespoons cornstarch
¼ teaspoon ground cinnamon
1 21-ounce can cherry pie filling
1½ cups frozen blueberries, do not thaw
1 teaspoon pure vanilla extract

Topping
1 egg white beaten in a small bowl with 1 teaspoon water
2 teaspoons granulated sugar

Preheat oven to 425°.

Crust: Line a 9-inch pie plate with one crust.

Filling: Mix sugar, cornstarch and cinnamon in a large bowl. Add cherry pie filling, blueberries and vanilla extract; mix well. Spoon mixture into prepared crust. Top with second crust; seal edges and flute. Cut three slits in top of crust to vent steam. Cover edges of crust with cooking foil.

Topping: Brush top crust with some of the egg mixture; discard remaining mixture. Sprinkle with 2 teaspoons sugar. Bake 45–55 minutes or until crust is golden, removing foil during last 10 minutes. Remove from oven. Cool on a wire rack 2 hours before serving. Refrigerate leftovers.

Makes 8 servings.

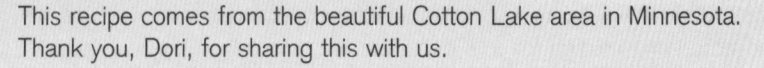

CHERRY-BANANA PIE

This recipe comes from the beautiful Cotton Lake area in Minnesota.
Thank you, Dori, for sharing this with us.

1 9-inch baked pie shell

1 16-ounce can pitted red cherries, undrained
1 cup granulated sugar
3 tablespoons cornstarch
1 tablespoon butter
½ teaspoon ground cinnamon, or as desired
1 teaspoon pure vanilla extract
2 ripe bananas

Mix cherries, sugar and cornstarch in a medium saucepan. Stir over medium heat
until mixture thickens and boils; boil 1 minute stirring constantly. Stir in butter; cool.
Stir in cinnamon and vanilla. Slice bananas, and layer in baked pie shell. Pour cooled
filling over bananas; chill until set. Serve with whipped cream. Refrigerate leftovers.

Makes 8 servings.

CHERRY DREAM PIE

A quick pie to prepare...make your own graham cracker crust if desired.

1 6-ounce packaged graham cracker pie crust

3 egg yolks
1 14-ounce can sweetened condensed milk
⅓ cup fresh lemon juice
1 teaspoon pure vanilla extract

1 21-ounce can cherry pie filling, chilled
sweetened whipped cream

Preheat oven to 350°.

Beat egg yolks in a medium bowl. Stir in sweetened condensed milk, lemon juice and vanilla extract. Pour mixture into prepared crust. Bake 8 minutes. Remove from oven. Refrigerate. Chill well before serving. When serving, top each serving with chilled cherry pie filling and sweetened whipped cream. Refrigerate leftovers.

Makes 8 servings.

CHERRY-TOPPED FUDGE PIE

Cherries and sour cream top this fudge pie.

pastry for single crust 9-inch pie

Filling
- **¾ cup butter**
- **1 cup granulated sugar, divided**
- **6 tablespoons unsweetened cocoa powder**
- **⅔ cup ground blanched almonds**
- **2 tablespoons all-purpose flour**
- **3 eggs, separated**
- **2 tablespoons cold water**

Topping
- **1 cup dairy sour cream**
- **2 tablespoons granulated sugar**
- **½ teaspoon pure vanilla extract**
- **⅔ cup canned cherry pie filling**

Glaze
- **1 teaspoon butter**
- **1 teaspoon unsweetened cocoa powder**
- **1 teaspoon cold water**
- **¼ teaspoon pure vanilla extract**
- **¼ cup powdered sugar**

Preheat oven to 350°.
Line a 9-inch pie pan with one single unbaked pie crust; flute edges.

Filling: Melt butter over medium heat. Stir in ¾ cup sugar and cocoa. Remove from heat; cool 5 minutes. Stir in almonds and flour. Beat in egg yolks, one at a time. Stir in water. Beat egg whites in a small bowl until foamy. Gradually beat in ¼ cup sugar to form soft peaks. Stir in chocolate mixture until just mixed. Pour into crust. Bake 40–50 minutes or until a wooden pick inserted in center comes out clean. Cool 5 minutes.

Topping: Mix sour cream, sugar and vanilla; spread evenly over warm pie filling. Top with spoonfuls of cherry pie filling. Return to oven; bake 5 minutes.

Glaze: Microwave butter on High. Stir in cocoa and water. Microwave, stirring often, until mixture thickens slightly. Stir in vanilla and powdered sugar; beat with a wire whisk until smooth. Drizzle over pie. Serve warm. Refrigerate leftovers.

Makes 8 servings.

CHERRY-TOPPED PINEAPPLE PIE

Add more whipped cream...if desired.

1½ cups flake coconut
¾ cup graham cracker crumbs
⅓ cup butter, melted

2 packages 4-serving size vanilla flavor instant pudding mix
2 cups whole milk
1 cup dairy sour cream
1 teaspoon pure vanilla extract
1 8-ounce can crushed pineapple, drained
1 cup miniature marshmallows

½ cup whipped cream
12 fresh sweet cherries, pitted and cut in half

Preheat oven to 325°.

Mix coconut, graham cracker crumbs and melted butter in a bowl; press mixture onto bottom and up side of a 9-inch ungreased pie plate. Bake 8 minutes; cool.

Beat pudding mix and milk in a bowl 2 minutes or until well blended. Stir in sour cream, vanilla extract, pineapple and marshmallows. Spoon mixture into prepared crust. Chill in refrigerator 1 hour. Top with whipped cream and garnish with cherries. Refrigerate leftovers.

Makes 8 servings.

CHOCOLATE CHERRY CHEESECAKE PIE

Only the crust is baked in this pie.

Crust
1½ cups chocolate wafer crumbs
¼ cup butter, melted

1 8-ounce package cream cheese, softened
½ cup granulated sugar
2 tablespoons whole milk
1 teaspoon pure vanilla extract

1 1-ounce square unsweetened chocolate, melted
½ cup whipping cream, whipped
1 21-ounce can cherry pie filling

Preheat oven to 375°.

Crust: Mix chocolate wafer crumbs and butter in a small bowl. Press onto bottom of an ungreased 9-inch pie baking plate. Bake 8 minutes. Cool.

Beat cream cheese, sugar, milk and vanilla extract in a medium bowl until well blended. Divide mixture in half.

Stir chocolate in a bowl with half of the cream cheese mixture. Fold whipped cream into remaining cream cheese mixture.

Pour chocolate mixture into cooled crust. Top with half of cherry pie filling, then top with whipped cream mixture and remaining pie filling. Chill well before serving. Refrigerate leftovers.

Makes 8 servings.

CHOCOLATE CHIP CHERRY PIE

Chocolate chips in crust and topping.

Crust
½ cup semisweet chocolate chips
5 tablespoons butter
¾ cup uncooked rolled oats
¾ cup all-purpose flour
¼ cup brown sugar, packed

Topping
½ cup all-purpose flour
2 tablespoons brown sugar, packed
2 tablespoons uncooked rolled oats
3 tablespoons soft butter
¼ cup semisweet chocolate chips

Filling
1 16-ounce can cherry pie filling
1 16-ounce can tart water-packed red cherries
¼ teaspoon almond extract

Preheat oven to 350°.
Grease a 10-inch pie baking pan.

Crust: Melt chocolate chips and butter in a heavy saucepan over medium heat; remove from heat. Stir in oats, flour and brown sugar until well mixed. Press mixture into prepared pan. Bake 10 minutes. Remove from oven.

Filling: Mix cherry pie filling, tart cherries and almond extract in a bowl; spoon mixture into baked crust.

Topping: Mix flour, brown sugar and oats in a small bowl. Cut in butter until coarse crumbs form. Stir in chocolate chips. Sprinkle mixture evenly over filling. Return to oven. Bake 35 minutes. Cool. Refrigerate leftovers.

Makes 10 servings.

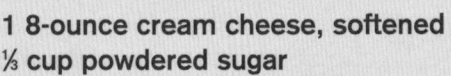

CHOCOLATE-COVERED CHERRY PIE

Chocolate, cheese, cherries and chocolate covered cherries in this pie.

2 cups semisweet
  chocolate chips
½ cup whipping cream
¼ cup butter or margarine,
  cut up
1 6-ounce purchased
  chocolate crumb pie crust
1 21-ounce can cherry pie filling

1 8-ounce cream cheese, softened
⅓ cup powdered sugar
1 large egg
1 teaspoon pure vanilla extract

16 maraschino cherries with stems,
  drained and pat dry with paper towel
2 cups thawed frozen nondairy whipped
  topping

Microwave chocolate chips and cream in a glass bowl at medium (50% power) 1–2 minutes or until chocolate begins to melt. Whisk in butter until smooth. Let cool, whisking occasionally, 5–10 minutes or until spreadable consistency. Spoon half the mixture into chocolate crust. Refrigerate remaining chocolate mixture. Spoon cherry pie filling over chocolate in crust; place on a baking sheet; set aside.

Beat cream cheese, powdered sugar, egg and vanilla with an electric mixer in a medium bowl until smooth. Pour mixture over cherry pie filling. Bake about 30 minutes or until center is set. Remove from oven; cool on a wire rack. Cover and chill 8 hours.

Heat refrigerated chocolate mixture in microwave at medium 1 minute; stir to a spreading consistency, reheating if necessary. Dip cherries in chocolate mixture; place on a plate lined with waxed paper; chill 15 minutes. Spread remaining chocolate mixture over top of pie. Garnish with whipped topping and chocolate cherries. Refrigerate leftovers.

Makes 8 servings.

FRESH CHERRY PIE

Serve warm or at room temperature.

pastry for 9-inch double pie crust

4 cups fresh pitted cherries
1⅛ cups granulated sugar
⅓ cup all-purpose flour
1 teaspoon almond extract
1 tablespoon butter, cut up

Preheat oven to 400°.

Line a 9-inch pie pan with one crust.

Mix cherries, sugar, flour and almond extract in a bowl; spoon into pie crust. Dot with butter. Cover with top crust. Seal edges. Cut several slits on top crust to vent steam. Bake about 40–55 minutes. Refrigerate leftovers.

Makes 6 servings.

ICE BOX PINEAPPLE-CHERRY PIE

No need to bake this pie...yummy.

Crust
1¼ cups graham cracker crumbs
¼ cup granulated sugar
¼ cup butter, melted and cooled slightly

Filling
1 8-ounce can crushed pineapple, undrained
1 8-ounce package cream cheese, softened
1 teaspoon pure vanilla extract
1 21-ounce can cherry pie filling

¼ cup powdered sugar
1 cup whipping cream

Crust: Mix all crust ingredients in a bowl; press into a 9-inch pie plate.

Filling: Drain pineapple, reserving two tablespoons syrup. Mix reserved syrup, cream cheese and vanilla extract in a bowl until well blended. Add ¼ cup pineapple and ½ cup cherry pie filling; mix lightly.

Gradually add sugar to whipping cream, beating until stiff peaks form. Fold into cream cheese mixture. Pour into prepared crust. Top with remaining pineapple and cherry pie filling. Refrigerate. Chill well before serving. Refrigerate leftovers.

Makes 8 servings.

LATTICE-TOPPED CHERRY PIE

A hint of orange in this good-looking cherry pie.

Crust
2 cups all-purpose flour
¼ teaspoon salt
⅔ cup cold butter
4–5 tablespoons cold water
milk
granulated sugar

Filling
1 cup granulated sugar
⅓ cup all-purpose flour
⅛ teaspoon salt
2 14-ounce cans red tart pitted cherries, drained
1 teaspoon freshly grated orange peel
1 teaspoon pure vanilla extract

Preheat oven to 400°.

Crust: Mix flour and salt. Cut in butter until coarse crumbs are formed. Stir in just enough water with a fork to moisten. Divide dough in half. Shape each half into a ball. Flatten slightly and wrap 1 ball in plastic food wrap; refrigerate. Roll out remaining ball on a floured surface into a 12-inch circle. Place into a 9-inch pie pan. Press firmly against bottom and sides. Trim crust to ½ inch from edge of pan.

Filling: Mix sugar, flour and salt. Gently stir in cherries, orange peel and vanilla extract. Spoon mixture into prepared crust.

Roll out remaining dough into an 11-inch circle. Cut into ten ½-inch strips. Place five strips across filling in pie pan 1 inch apart. Place remaining five strips at right angles 1 inch apart to strips already in place. Trim strips and fold edge of bottom crust over strips. Seal and crimp or flute edge. Brush with milk and sprinkle with sugar. Cover edge of crust with aluminum foil (cover strips with foil if browning too fast). Bake 50–60 minutes until crust is golden and filling bubbles in center. Remove foil the last 5 minutes of baking. Refrigerate leftovers.

Makes 8 servings.

NO-BAKE CHERRY-TOPPED CHEESECAKE PIE

Top with sweetened whipped cream when serving.

Crust
1¼ cups graham cracker crumbs
3 tablespoons granulated sugar
¼ cup butter, melted and cooled slightly

Filling
1 8-ounce package cream cheese, softened
1 14-ounce can sweetened condensed milk
⅓ cup lemon juice
1 teaspoon pure vanilla extract

1 21-ounce can cherry pie filing, chilled

Crust: Mix all crust ingredients in a bowl; press mixture into a 9-inch glass pie plate; chill.

Filling: Beat cream cheese with an electric mixer in a medium bowl until fluffy. Gradually beat in sweetened condensed milk until smooth. Stir in lemon juice and vanilla. Pour mixture into prepared crust. Immediately refrigerate. Chill well, at least 3 hours.

Top with cherry pie filling when serving. Refrigerate leftovers.

Makes 6 servings.

RHUBARB-CHERRY PIE

Rhubarb adds a tang to this cherry pie.

pastry for a double crust 9-inch pie

4 cups fresh rhubarb cut into ½-inch pieces
1 16-ounce can pitted tart cherries, drained
1½ cups granulated sugar
¼ cup quick-cooking tapioca
1 teaspoon pure vanilla extract
¼ teaspoon ground cinnamon mixed with
⅛ teaspoon ground nutmeg
1½ tablespoons cold butter cut up

Preheat oven to 400°.
Line a 9-inch baking pie plate with bottom crust.

Mix rhubarb, cherries, sugar, tapioca and vanilla in a large bowl; let stand 15 minutes. Pour mixture into prepared crust. Sprinkle with cinnamon mixture. Dot with butter.

With second crust, form a lattice for top. Place ½-inch wide strips of dough lengthwise spacing at 1-inch intervals. Fold back alternate strips; fold up as you weave crosswise strips over and under. Trim even along outer rim of pie; seal edges. Dampen edge of pie slightly with water and place extra strips around entire rim of pie, covering ends of lattice. Flute edge while pressing to seal. Bake 40–50 minutes or until filling is bubbly and crust golden. Refrigerate leftovers.

Makes 6 servings.

SAM'S CHERRY PIE

Cream cheese, pudding and cream in this pie...like Sam, unforgettable.

1 10-inch pastry shell baked in a glass pie plate

1 8-ounce package cream cheese
1 14-ounce can sweetened condensed milk

¾ cup cold water
1 4-serving size package instant vanilla flavor pudding mix
1 cup whipping cream, whipped in a medium bowl with
   2 tablespoons granulated sugar and 1 teaspoon pure
   vanilla extract
1 21-ounce can cherry pie filling, chilled

Beat cream cheese with an electric mix in a large bowl until fluffy. Gradually beat in sweetened condensed milk until smooth.

Beat in water and pudding mix on low speed until smooth. Chill mixture 10 minutes. Fold in whipped cream. Spread half the pudding mixture in prepared crust. Top with half the cherry pie filling. Repeat. Chill until set, about 2 hours. Refrigerate leftovers.

Makes 8 servings.

SANDRA'S SODA CRACKER CHERRY PIE

This recipe comes from Mississippi...thanks dear niece.

3 egg whites
½ teaspoon baking powder
1 cup granulated sugar
1 sleeve saltine crackers, finely crushed
½ cup chopped pecans

1 21-ounce can cherry pie filling
sweetened whipped cream

Preheat oven to 325°.
Spray a 9-inch baking pie plate with vegetable cooking spray.

Beat egg whites with an electric mixer in a large bowl until fluffy. Beat in baking powder. Gradually beat in sugar until stiff. Fold in crackers and pecans. Spread mixture evenly onto bottom and up sides of prepared pie plate. Bake 15 minutes. Remove from oven. Cool completely, then chill.

Top each serving with cherry pie filling and sweetened whipped cream when serving. Refrigerate leftovers.

Makes 8 servings.

SOUR CREAM FRESH CHERRY PIE

Serve chilled or at room temperature.

2 cups pitted fresh cherries
1 8-inch unbaked pie crust
1 8-inch unbaked pie crust, cut into strips for top of pie

3 eggs
¾ cup dairy sour cream
½ cup sugar (or more if cherries are tart)
¼ teaspoon salt
¼ teaspoon almond extract

Preheat oven to 400°.

Place cherries into one unbaked pie crust.

Beat eggs in a bowl. Add sour cream and sugar; beat until thickened. Stir in salt and almond extract. Pour mixture over cherries.

Top with strips forming a lattice pattern. Bake 25–35 minutes. Refrigerate leftovers.

Makes 6 servings.

TRIPLE CHERRY PIE

Top with a scoop of vanilla ice cream, of course.

pastry for a double crust 9-inch pie

2½ cups pitted fresh sweet cherries
2½ cups pitted frozen tart cherries
½ cup pitted dried tart cherries
¾ cup granulated sugar
2 tablespoons quick-cooking tapioca
½ teaspoon almond extract
¼ teaspoon ground nutmeg

1 tablespoon butter, cut up

Preheat oven to 375°.

Mix cherries, sugar, tapioca, almond extract and nutmeg in a large glass bowl. Let stand 15 minutes.

Line one pie crust into a 9-inch pie baking plate. Fill with cherry mixture. Dot with butter. Cut one pie crust into 6 strips 1 inch wide by 10 inches long. Weave strips into a lattice pattern over cherries; trim and crimp with edges of crust. Bake one hour or until filling is bubbly and crust golden. Cover crust with foil if browning too fast. Remove from oven. Cool slightly before serving. Refrigerate leftovers.

Makes 8 servings.

WALNUT CARAMEL CHERRY PIE

Serve this delicious pie topped with sweetened whipped cream.

Crust
1½ cups all-purpose flour
½ teaspoon salt
¼ teaspoon baking powder
3 tablespoons cold butter,
 cut up
2 tablespoons solid shortening
4–5 tablespoons ice
 cold water

Filling
1¼ cups pitted dried tart cherries, chopped
½ cup ruby port wine
⅔ cup golden brown sugar, packed
⅔ cup light corn syrup
3 large eggs
4 tablespoons butter, melted and cooled
1½ teaspoons pure vanilla extract
1 cup walnuts, toasted and chopped

Crust: Mix flour, salt and baking powder in a food processor until blended. Cut in butter and shortening using on-off pulse until mixture resembles coarse meal. Add 4 tablespoons water; process just until moist clumps form. Add more water a little at a time if dough is too dry. Form into a ball; flatten slightly and wrap into food plastic wrap. Chill 30 minutes.

Filling: Boil cherries and wine in a heavy small saucepan, stirring often, until wine is absorbed. Remove from heat; cool completely. Beat brown sugar, syrup, eggs, melted butter and vanilla in a large bowl with an electric mixer until well blended. Stir in walnuts and cherries.

Preheat oven to 350°.
Roll dough out on a floured surface to an 11-inch circle; place into a 9-inch glass pie baking plate. Fold overhang under and crimp edges. Pour filling into crust. Bake about 50 minutes or until filling is brown and just set in center. Cool completely. Refrigerate leftovers.

Makes 8 servings.

YOGURT CHOCOLATE CHERRY FROZEN PIE

Garnish with fresh sweet cherries when serving.

40 chocolate wafers
2 tablespoons granulated sugar
2 tablespoons solid margarine, melted
1 large egg white

4 cups vanilla frozen yogurt
1 cup chopped pitted sweet cherries
½ cup mini semisweet chocolate chips

½ cup black cherry preserves, melted

Preheat oven to 350°.
Coat a 9-inch pie plate with cooking spray.

Process chocolate wafers in a food process until crumbly. Add sugar, margarine and egg white. Pulse just until moist. Press mixture evenly into prepared pie plate. Bake 8 minutes. Remove from oven; cool on a wire rack 15 minutes, then freeze 30 minutes.

Spoon yogurt into a very large bowl. Stir in cherries and chocolate chips; freeze just until set but not firm, about 30 minutes.

Spread preserves over bottom of prepared crust. Spoon yogurt mixture evenly over preserves; freeze until set. Cover with food plastic wrap; freeze until firm, about 6 hours. Remove from freezer and let stand in the refrigerator 30 minutes before serving. Freeze leftovers.

Makes 8 servings.

YVONNE'S CHERRY CHEESECAKE PIE

My friend, Yvonne, lives in Rochester, New York. She loves cheesecake...topped with cherries, of course.

Crust
1½ cups graham cracker crumbs
¼ cup granulated sugar
¼ cup butter, melted and cooled slightly

Filling
2 8-ounce packages cream cheese, softened
½ cup granulated sugar
2 eggs
1 cup dairy sour cream
2 tablespoons melted butter
1 teaspoon pure vanilla extract

Topping
¾ cup pitted dried tart cherries
1-pound bag frozen pitted Bing cherries, thawed, drained, juice reserved
½ cup cherry jam
2 tablespoons brandy or orange juice
1 tablespoon cornstarch

Preheat oven to 400°.
Crust: Mix crust ingredients and press mixture onto bottom and up sides of a 9-inch deep-dish pie plate. Bake 6 minutes. Cool completely.

Reduce heat to 325°.
Filling: Beat cream cheese with an electric mixer until fluffy. Beat in sugar, eggs, sour cream, butter and vanilla until well blended. Pour into baked crust. Bake until center is set, 35–45 minutes. Chill well before serving. Top with cherry topping as desired when serving. Refrigerate leftovers.

Topping: Bring dried cherries and reserved juice to a boil in a medium saucepan. Remove from heat; let steep 20 minutes. Mix cherry jam, brandy and cornstarch until blended; stir into dried cherry mixture. Add thawed cherries. Bring to a boil, stirring, until thickened, about 1 minute. Chill. Store in refrigerator.

Makes 8 servings.

BAKED CHERRY TURNOVERS

Refrigerated piecrust is used for this tasty treat!

1 15-ounce package refrigerated pie crusts
1 cup canned cherry pie filling
¼ cup chopped pecans, toasted
½ teaspoon pure vanilla extract

1 tablespoon granulated sugar
¼ teaspoon ground cinnamon

Preheat oven to 425°.
Lightly grease a baking sheet.

Cut each piecrust into 6 wedges.
Mix pie filling, pecans and vanilla in a small bowl; spoon mixture evenly in center of 6 wedges. Top with remaining 6 wedges. Moisten edges of pie crust with water, pressing to seal, then crimp edges with a fork. Place on prepared baking sheet. Bake 12–14 minutes. Remove from oven.

Mix sugar and cinnamon in a cup; sprinkle evenly over warm turnovers. Serve warm. Refrigerate leftovers.

Makes 6 turnovers.

Fried Turnovers: Heat 1-inch depth corn oil in heavy Dutch oven over medium-high heat. Fry turnovers in batches, in hot oil 3–4 minutes or until golden, turning once. Drain on paper towels. Refrigerate leftovers.

CHERRY BISMARCKS

Cherry preserves fill these home-made bismarcks.

⅓ cup butter
½ cup granulated sugar
1 teaspoon salt
1 cup whole milk

1 package active dry yeast
¼ cup warm water (105–115°)
3 eggs, lightly beaten
5½–6½ cups all-purpose flour, divided

cherry preserves
vegetable oil
granulated sugar

Mix butter, sugar and salt in a large mixing bowl. Heat milk in a small saucepan until very warm; pour over butter mixture. Cool to lukewarm.

Dissolve yeast in warm water in a small bowl; let stand 5 minutes. Add to lukewarm mixture in large bowl. Add eggs and 3 cups flour. Beat until smooth. Add additional flour to make a stiff dough. Knead dough on a lightly-floured surface until smooth and elastic, about 10 minutes.

Divide dough into thirds. Roll one part at a time to ¼-inch thickness. Cut into 3-inch rounds. Place a heaping teaspoonful cherry preserves on half the dough rounds. Cover with remaining dough rounds. Moisten edges with cold water and press edges to seal. Place on floured baking sheets. Cover with a clean tea towel. Let rise until doubled, about 30 minutes.

Heat oil to 360° in a deep-fryer. Fry bismarcks about 2 minutes, then turn and fry until golden, about 2 minutes. Drain on paper towels. Make a small slit on top; roll in granulated sugar.

Makes about 30.

CHERRY CHEESE DANISH DESSERT

Serve this treat for a special breakfast.

2 8-ounce cans refrigerated crescent dinner rolls

2 8-ounce packages cream cheese, softened
¾ cup powdered sugar
1 egg white
1 teaspoon pure vanilla extract
1 21-ounce can cherry pie filling

Topping
3 tablespoons whole milk
¾ cup powdered sugar
¼ teaspoon pure vanilla extract

Preheat oven to 350°.
Grease a 13x9-inch baking pan.

Unroll 1 can crescent dough into 2 long rectangles. Place in prepared pan and press onto bottom to form a crust. Press seams firmly to seal.

Beat cream cheese, ¾ cup powdered sugar, egg white and vanilla extract with an electric mixer on medium speed until well blended. Spread mixture over crust. Cover evenly with pie filling. Unroll remaining can of crescent dough and separate into 2 long rectangles. Pat out to form a 13x9-inch rectangle; press seams firmly together to seal. Place over pie filling. Bake about 25 minutes or until golden. Remove from oven; cool slightly.

Topping: Beat milk, ¾ cup powdered sugar and vanilla in a small bowl until well blended; drizzle over warm Danish. Refrigerate leftovers.

Makes 24 servings.

Used with permission from the Cherry Marketing Institute.

CHERRY PAN PASTRY

Best served warm but good cool too.

Filling
½ cup granulated sugar
¼ cup butter, softened
1 teaspoon pure vanilla extract
¼ teaspoon almond extract
¼ cup all-purpose flour
½ cup flaked coconut
½ cup chopped macadamia nuts
or almonds
½ cup white baking chips
½ cup dried cherries

Crust
1 15-ounce can refrigerated pie
crusts, softened as directed
on package
1 egg, beaten

Glaze
½ cup powdered sugar
½ teaspoon pure vanilla extract
3 teaspoons fresh orange juice

Preheat oven to 375°.

Filling: Beat sugar, butter and vanilla and almond extract in a medium bowl until fluffy. Beat in flour. Stir in coconut, nuts, chips and cherries.

Crust: Unfold 1 crust onto an ungreased baking sheet; press out fold lines. Spread filling mixture within 1 inch of edges. Brush edges with beaten egg. Unfold 1 crust and press out lines; place over filling. Press and crimp edges to seal. Brush top with beaten egg. Bake 18–25 minutes or until golden. Remove from oven. Cool 15 minutes.

Glaze: Whisk all glaze ingredients in a bowl to a drizzling consistency. Drizzle over pastry. Cut into wedges. Refrigerate leftovers.

Makes 1 dozen.

EASY CHERRY STOLLEN

Sprinkle with powdered sugar when serving.

2¼ cups all-purpose flour
½ cup granulated sugar
1½ teaspoons baking powder
¼ teaspoon salt

½ cup cold butter
1 cup whole milk ricotta cheese
½ cup red candied cherries, coarsely chopped
½ cup tart dried cherries, coarsely chopped
⅓ cup pecans, toasted, chopped
1 teaspoon pure vanilla extract
½ teaspoon freshly grated lemon peel
1 large egg plus 1 egg yolk

Preheat oven to 325°.
Grease a large baking sheet.

Mix flour, sugar, baking powder and salt in a large bowl. Cut in butter with a pastry blender until fine crumbs form. Stir in ricotta until moistened. Stir in remaining ingredients until well mixed.

Gently knead dough on a floured surface 2–3 times. Roll out with a floured rolling pin into a 10x8-inch oval. Fold lengthwise almost in half, letting bottom dough extend about 1 inch beyond edge of top dough. Place on prepared baking sheet. Bake about 1 hour or until a wooden pick inserted in center comes out clean. Remove from baking sheet; cool completely on a wire rack. Refrigerate leftovers.

Makes 12 servings.

KOLACHES WITH CHERRY FILLING

Dust with powdered sugar when serving and enjoy!

4–4½ cups all-purpose flour, divided
1 package active dry yeast
½ teaspoon ground nutmeg
1 cup whole milk
½ cup butter
¼ cup granulated sugar
1 teaspoon salt
2 eggs
1 teaspoon pure vanilla extract

1 egg beaten in a small bowl with
  1 tablespoon milk

Cherry Filling
2 cups pitted, chopped cherries
¾ cup granulated sugar
¼ cup cornstarch
½ cup water
½ teaspoon vanilla

Cherry Filling: Bring cherries and sugar to a boil. Cook 3 minutes. Mix cornstarch with water until dissolved; stir into cherries and cook until thickened. Stir in vanilla; cool.

Mix 2 cups flour, yeast and nutmeg; set aside. Stir and heat milk, butter, ¼ cup sugar and salt until warm and butter melts (120°–130°). Add milk mixture, 2 eggs and vanilla to flour mixture. Beat with an electric mixer on low speed 30 seconds, scraping sides of bowl. Beat on high 3 minutes. Turn onto a floured surface; knead in enough flour to form soft smooth elastic dough, about 5 minutes.

Shape dough into a ball; place in a greased bowl, turning once. Cover; let rise in a warm place until double in bulk, about 1 hour. Punch dough down. Divide in half. Cover and let rest on a floured surface 10 minutes. Roll each half into a 12x8-inch rectangle. Cut each rectangle into six 4x4-inch squares. Spoon a rounded teaspoon of cherry filling onto the center of each. Brush the corners with water. Draw corners up and press together. Place on greased baking sheets 2 inches apart. Cover; let rise until double.

Brush with egg mixture. Bake in a preheated 375° oven 12–15 minutes or until golden. Cool on a wire rack.

Makes 1 dozen.

Gelatin Salads
Other Salads
Soups

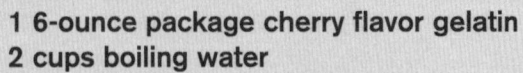

DALI'S CHERRY SALAD

Variation: Add ¼ cup chopped pecans.

1 6-ounce package cherry flavor gelatin
2 cups boiling water
3 ounces cream cheese, cut up
1 21-ounce can cherry pie filling
¾ cup dairy sour cream
1 large ripe banana, sliced
1½ cups miniature marshmallows

Stir gelatin and boiling water in an 11x7-inch glass baking dish until completely dissolved. Stir in cream cheese. Stir in pie filling and sour cream. Stir in banana and marshmallows. Refrigerate until set. Store in refrigerator.

Makes 12 servings.

CHERRY COLA SALAD

A good salad for special holidays.

1 16-ounce can pitted Bing cherries, drained, reserve juice
reserved cherry juice and enough water to measure 1½ cups
1 cup cola-flavored carbonated beverage
1 6-ounce package black cherry flavor gelatin

1 8-ounce package cream cheese, softened
¼ cup mayonnaise
1 15-ounce can crushed pineapple, drained
1 cup chopped pecans

Bring cherry juice mixture and cola to a boil a saucepan; pour into a bowl. Add black cherry gelatin; stir until dissolved.

Mix cream cheese and mayonnaise in a small bowl until blended; stir into hot gelatin mixture. Refrigerate. Chill until slightly thickened. Stir in cherries, pineapple and pecans. Pour mixture into a 6-quart mold sprayed with nonstick cooking spray. Refrigerate until firm. Store in refrigerator.

Makes 10 servings.

CHERRY-PINEAPPLE SALAD

Variation: Spoon into 8 individual dessert dishes.

1 3-ounce package cherry flavor gelatin
1 cup boiling water
½ cup ice cubes
1 21-ounce can cherry pie filling
1 20-ounce can crushed pineapple, drained
1 cup miniature marshmallows
sweetened whipped cream

Stir gelatin and water in a bowl until dissolved. Stir in ice cubes until melted. Chill until slightly thickened. Whip with a wire whisk. Stir in cherry pie filling, pineapple and marshmallows. Spoon mixture into a 6-cup mold or glass bowl. Refrigerate until set. Top with sweetened whipped cream when serving. Store in refrigerator.

Makes 8 servings.

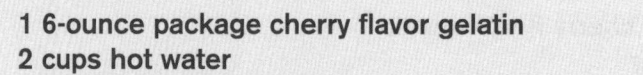

FRESH CHERRY GELATIN SALAD

Cherry juice and fresh cherries...a lot of salad!

1 6-ounce package cherry flavor gelatin
2 cups hot water
1 cup cold water
2 teaspoons fresh lemon juice
2 tablespoons cherry juice

1 cup dairy sour cream
2 cups fresh Bing cherries, pitted and halved
¼ cup chopped toasted almonds

Dissolve gelatin in hot water in a bowl. Stir in cold water and lemon juice.
To one cup of mixture add the cherry juice; pour mixture into a two-quart mold.
Chill until set.

Chill remaining gelatin mixture until partially set, then whip until fluffy. Fold in sour cream, cherries and almonds. Pour over first gelatin mixture. Refrigerate and chill well before serving. Unmold onto a chilled serving plate lined with lettuce. Refrigerate leftovers.

Makes 8 servings.

LOLA'S CHERRY SALAD

Sour cream and almonds in this cherry salad.

1 6-ounce package cherry flavor gelatin
2 cups boiling water

2 cups dairy sour cream
2 cups pitted dark sweet cherries, halved
½ cup slivered blanched almonds

Stir cherry gelatin and boiling water in a large bowl until dissolved; cool.

When cool, beat in sour cream until smooth. Stir in cherries and almonds.
Pour mixture into a 7-cup mold or glass bowl. Refrigerate until set. Store
in refrigerator.

Makes 10 servings.

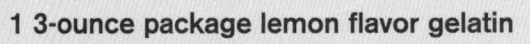

PINEAPPLE-CHERRY GELATIN SALAD

Variation: Lime flavor gelatin instead of lemon flavor.

1 3-ounce package lemon flavor gelatin
1 cup boiling water
1 20-ounce can crushed pineapple
½ cup cottage cheese
1 cup sweetened whipped cream
¼ cup maraschino cherries, chopped
¼ cup chopped blanched toasted almonds

Dissolve gelatin in boiling water in a bowl. Drain pineapple; add ½ cup syrup to gelatin. Chill until very thick, about 1½ hours.

Fold in remaining ingredients. Pour into individual molds or a 9x5x2-inch loaf pan. Refrigerate and chill until firm. Store in refrigerator.

Makes 8 servings.

RASPBERRY-LEMON-CHERRY SALAD

Variation: Cherry flavored gelatin instead of raspberry.

1 3-ounce package raspberry flavor gelatin
1 cup boiling water
1 21-ounce can tart cherry pie filling

1 3-ounce lemon flavor gelatin
1 cup boiling water

4 ounces cream cheese, softened
⅓ cup mayonnaise
1 8-ounce can crushed pineapple, undrained
½ cup heavy cream, whipped
1 cup miniature marshmallows
2 tablespoons chopped pecans

Stir raspberry gelatin and 1 cup boiling water in a bowl until dissolved. Stir in cherry pie filling; pour mixture into a 13x9-x 2-inch glass baking dish. Refrigerate until firm.

Stir lemon gelatin and 1 cup boiling water in a bowl until dissolved; set aside. Beat cream cheese and mayonnaise in a large bowl until blended. Gradually stir in lemon gelatin mixture. Stir in pineapple. Fold in whipped cream and marshmallows. Spread on top of firm raspberry gelatin mixture in glass dish. Refrigerate until set. Sprinkle with pecans. Store in refrigerator.

Makes 12 servings.

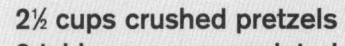

TERRI'S CHERRY PRETZEL SALAD

Serve topped with sweetened whipped cream or thawed whipped topping.

2½ cups crushed pretzels
3 tablespoons granulated sugar
¾ cup butter or margarine, melted

1 8-ounce cream cheese, softened
1 cup granulated sugar
1 teaspoon pure vanilla extract
1 cup whipped cream, whipped, or one 8-ounce container frozen
   nondairy whipped topping, thawed

1 6-ounce package strawberry flavor gelatin
2 cups boiling water
8 ounces pitted frozen sweet cherries
1 10-ounce package frozen strawberries

Preheat oven to 350°.

Mix pretzels, 3 tablespoons sugar and butter in a 13x9x2-inch baking pan; press mixture evenly. Bake 9 minutes; remove from oven and cool completely in pan on a wire rack.

Beat cream cheese, 1 cup sugar and vanilla in a large bowl; fold in whipped cream or thawed topping. Spread over cooled crust in pan.

Dissolve gelatin in boiling water. Stir in frozen cherries and strawberries. Refrigerate and cool until partially set; pour over cream cheese layer. Refrigerate uncovered 8 hours. Store in refrigerator.

Makes 15 servings.

BUTTER LETTUCE CHERRY SALAD

Serve with freshly baked rolls...buttered of course.

8 slices bacon, diced

3 tablespoons mayonnaise
2 tablespoons white wine vinegar
½ cup vegetable oil
1 cup crumbled Roquefort cheese (about 4 ounces)
salt and black pepper to taste

2 heads butter lettuce, torn into large pieces
½ cup dried tart cherries (about 3 ounces)

Cook bacon in a heavy skillet over medium-high heat until brown and crisp; drain on paper towels.

Whisk mayonnaise and vinegar in a medium bowl. Gradually whisk in oil. Whisk in cheese. Season with salt and black pepper.

Toss lettuce, ¼ cup cherries and half of crisp drained bacon in a salad bowl with enough dressing to coat. Place equal portions on 6 individual salad plates. Top with remaining cherries and bacon. Refrigerate leftovers.

Makes 6 servings.

CHEERY CHERRY CHICKEN SALAD

Serve this main-course salad along with soup and warm bread.

4 cups cubed cooked chicken
1 cup pitted dried tart cherries
½ cup chopped walnuts
6 green onions, sliced

1 cup mayonnaise
½ cup plain yogurt
2 tablespoons fresh lemon juice
1 teaspoon dried oregano
freshly ground pepper to taste
salt to taste
lettuce leaves

Mix chicken, cherries, walnuts and onions in a large bowl.

Mix mayonnaise, yogurt, lemon juice, oregano, pepper and salt in a small bowl. Pour mixture over chicken mixture; mix well. Cover and refrigerate until chilled, about 2 hours. Serve on lettuce leaves. Refrigerate leftovers.

Makes 4 servings.

CHERRY CHICKEN SALAD

Creamy ginger dressing tops this salad.

Salad
2 cups pitted fresh sweet cherries
1 11-ounce can mandarin orange segments, drained
1½ cups diced cooked chicken
½ cup chopped celery
⅓ cup toasted slivered almonds
lettuce

Ginger Dressing
½ cup mayonnaise
1 tablespoon fresh lemon juice
1 teaspoon soy sauce
¼ teaspoon grated fresh ginger

Toss all salad ingredients except lettuce in a large bowl until well mixed.

Mix all dressing ingredients in a bowl; store in refrigerator.

Serve salad on lettuce-lined plates. Top each serving with ginger salad dressing. Refrigerate leftovers.

Makes 4 servings.

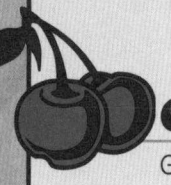

CHERRY FRUIT SALAD

Great for serving along with cold meat sandwiches.

1 21-ounce can cherry pie filling
1 20-ounce can pineapple chunks, undrained
3 ripe bananas, sliced
1 cup miniature marshmallows
1 cup chopped pecans
1 tablespoon mayonnaise

Mix all ingredients in a large serving bowl. Chill before serving. Store leftovers in refrigerator.

Makes 10 servings.

CHERRY SLAW

Garnish with pine nuts when serving.

Slaw
4 cups shredded green cabbage
3 cups sweet cherries, pitted and halved
2 cups torn fresh spinach leaves
1 cup shredded jicama
1 cup shredded carrot
½ cup snipped fresh cilantro
½ cup diced red onion
1 avocado, peeled and diced

Dressing
2 tablespoons extra virgin olive oil
½ teaspoon lime zest
2 tablespoons fresh lime juice
2 tablespoons frozen lime juice concentrate, thawed
1 fresh jalapeno pepper, seeded and minced
¼ teaspoon each chili powder and cumin
¼ teaspoon salt

Mix all slaw ingredients in a large bowl.

Mix all dressing ingredients in small saucepan; bring to a boil. Pour mixture over salad mixture in bowl; toss to coat. Refrigerate leftovers.

Makes 6 servings.

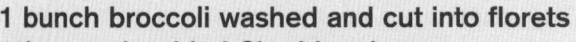

CHERRY SUNFLOWER SALAD

Beautiful sunflowers...seeds in a delicious salad.

1 bunch broccoli washed and cut into florets
1½ cups shredded Cheddar cheese
6 strips bacon, cooked crisp and crumbled
1 cup pitted dried cherries
¾ cup shelled sunflower seeds
½ cup chopped onion

½ cup mayonnaise
½ cup plain yogurt
2 tablespoons red wine vinegar
1 teaspoon sugar, optional

Mix first six ingredients in a large bowl.

Mix mayonnaise, yogurt, vinegar and sugar in a small bowl until blended. Pour over broccoli mixture in bowl; toss to coat. Serve or refrigerate.

Makes 6 servings.

CHERRY WHIPPED SALAD

Recipe courtesy of Pam Johnson, Burnsville, Minnesota.

**1 16-ounce can pitted Bing cherries in juice, drained,
  reserving juice**
1 cup cold water
reserved cherry juice
1 3-ounce package cherry flavor gelatin
1 cup miniature marshmallows
½ cup whipping cream, whipped
¾ cup coarsely chopped walnuts, optional

Bring water and cherry juice to a boil in a saucepan. Dissolve gelatin in boiling water mixture. Stir in marshmallows. Refrigerate until partially set. Beat, then fold in whipped cream, drained cherries and nuts. Spoon mixture into a mold or bowl. Chill. Store in refrigerator.

Makes 6 servings.

CHICKEN CHERRY PASTA SALAD

This is a good luncheon salad. Serve with rolls...and butter of course.

1 tablespoon corn oil
1 (2.25 pound) package frozen boneless skinless chicken breast strips

1 16-ounce package dry shell pasta
¾ cup thinly sliced celery
¾ cup chopped red onion
1 5-ounce package pitted dried cherries

1¼ cups mayonnaise
1¼ cups creamy style poppy seed dressing
1½ teaspoons salt
¼ teaspoon freshly ground black pepper
4 cups baby spinach, stems removed
1 cup chopped walnuts, toasted
curly leaf lettuce

Heat corn oil over medium-high heat in a nonstick skillet. Stir and cook chicken until all sides are brown and juices run clear, about 15 minutes. Remove from skillet; cool and cut into cubes.

Cook pasta according to package directions. Rinse with cold water. Drain well. Place in a large bowl. Add celery, onion and cherries.

Mix mayonnaise and poppy seed dressing in a small bowl; fold ¾ cup into pasta mixture. Refrigerate remaining dressing mixture. Cover and refrigerate salad several hours. When serving, fold in spinach and walnuts, adding reserved dressing as needed. Serve over lettuce.

Makes 8 servings.

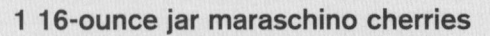

FROZEN CHERRY FRUIT SALAD

Almost dessert...serve on a lettuce leaf.

1 16-ounce jar maraschino cherries
1 8-ounce package cream cheese, softened
1 20-ounce can crushed pineapple, undrained
1 11-ounce can mandarin oranges, drained
2½ cups miniature marshmallows
1 8-ounce container frozen nondairy whipped topping, thawed

Drain cherries, reserve ¼ cup juice; set aside.

Beat cream cheese and pineapple in a medium bowl with an electric mixer on medium speed until combined, about 3 minutes. Stir in mandarin oranges, cherries and reserved ¼ cup juice. Fold in marshmallows and whipped topping. Spread mixture evenly into a 13x9x 2-inch glass baking dish. Freeze until firm, about 12 hours. Store in freezer.

Makes 12 servings.

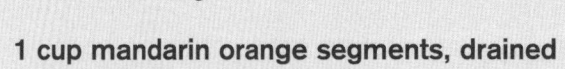

JOHN'S EASY SIDE SALAD

Great with hot dogs.

1 cup mandarin orange segments, drained
1 cup flaked coconut
1 cup miniature marshmallows
1 cup dairy sour cream
1 cup pecans, chopped or leave whole
1 10-ounce jar maraschino cherries, drained

Mix all ingredients in a glass bowl. Chill. Refrigerate leftovers.

Makes 4 servings.

LEMONY FRESH FRUIT SALAD

Fresh pineapple, grapes, mango and cherries in this tasty fruit salad.

3 tablespoons granulated sugar
½ cup cold water
2 teaspoons freshly grated lemon peel
1 teaspoon freshly grated orange peel
1 tablespoon fresh lemon juice
1 ripe pineapple, peeled, cored and cut into ¾-inch pieces
1½ pounds red seedless grapes
1 pound fresh Bing cherries, stemmed and pitted
1 mango, peeled, pitted and diced

Bring sugar and water to a boil in a small saucepan over medium-high heat. Stir until sugar is dissolved. Add lemon and orange peel; cool to room temperature, then place in a large bowl.

Stir in remaining ingredients. Cover and refrigerate up to 6 hours. Store in refrigerator.

Makes 12 servings.

PECAN CHERRY SALAD

Serve with hard rolls...and butter of course.

Balsamic Vinegar Dressing
½ cup extra virgin olive oil
⅓ cup balsamic vinegar
3 tablespoons soy sauce
1 tablespoon Dijon-style mustard
1 tablespoon snipped fresh parsley
1 teaspoon black pepper

6 cups torn mixed salad greens
⅓ cup balsamic vinegar dressing
½ cup dried cherries
½ cup toasted pecan halves
grated or shaved Parmesan cheese

Balsamic Vinegar Dressing: Whisk together all dressing ingredients. Pour in a tightly covered jar. Shake well. Store in refrigerator up to 1 week.

Toss greens in a large bowl with ⅓ cup balsamic dressing. Place equal portions on chilled salad plates. Top each salad with 2 tablespoons cherries, 2 tablespoons pecans and cheese as desired.

Makes 4 servings.

SMOKED TURKEY CHERRY SALAD

A nice luncheon salad.

1 cup cubed smoked turkey
1 head Romaine lettuce, coarsely chopped
½ cup crumbled feta cheese
¼ cup diced green onion, include some green tops
1 11-ounce can mandarin orange segments, drained
⅔ cup pitted Bing cherries, halved

Vinaigrette
⅓ cup extra virgin olive oil
2 tablespoons balsamic vinegar
1 tablespoon grained mustard
1 teaspoon honey
¼ teaspoon salt
freshly ground black pepper to taste

Toss first five ingredients in a large salad bowl.

Whisk all vinaigrette ingredients in a bowl; refrigerate.

To serve, toss cherries with one tablespoon vinaigrette in a small bowl. Add remaining vinaigrette to salad; toss. Arrange salad on individual salad plates. Garnish with cherries. Refrigerate leftovers.

Makes 4 servings.

SPINACH SALAD WITH CHERRIES

Cherries add a little tang to this spinach salad.

Salad
5 cups stemmed torn spinach leaves
1 cup pineapple chunks
½ cup dried tart cherries
½ cup thinly sliced red onion

Dressing
¼ cup extra virgin olive oil
¼ cup red wine vinegar
2 teaspoons honey
⅛ teaspoon freshly ground pepper

feta cheese

Mix all salad ingredients in a large salad bowl.

Whisk all dressing ingredients in a small bowl. Spoon over salad in bowl; toss to coat. Serve topped with feta cheese as desired.

Makes 4 servings.

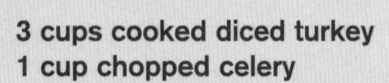

TURKEY CHERRY SALAD

Serve with warm rolls.

3 cups cooked diced turkey
1 cup chopped celery
½ cup pitted dried cherries
½ cup chopped onion
2 hard boiled eggs, chopped

½ cup mayonnaise
1 tablespoon fresh lemon juice
¼ teaspoon salt
freshly ground black pepper to taste

Mix turkey, celery, cherries, onion and eggs in a medium bowl.

Mix mayonnaise, lemon juice, salt and black pepper in a small bowl until blended; stir mixture into turkey mixture. Chill. Serve on bed of mixed lettuce leaves. Refrigerate leftovers.

Makes 4 servings.

FRESH CHERRY SOUP

Garnish each serving with a sprig of fresh mint.

1½ pounds sweet cherries, pitted
1 cup dry red wine
1 cup cold water
1 tablespoon light brown sugar

6 tablespoons reduced-fat sour cream
3 tablespoons fresh lemon juice
¼ teaspoon pure almond extract
4 rounded tablespoons lemon sorbet

Bring cherries, wine, water and brown sugar to a boil in a medium saucepan. Reduce heat to low; simmer 10 minutes. Remove from heat; cool 15 minutes. Remove cherries; puree in a food processor. Pour into a glass bowl along with mixture in saucepan. Cover and chill 2 hours.

Add sour cream, lemon juice and almond extract; whisk until smooth. Ladle soup into bowls; top with lemon sorbet. Serve immediately. Refrigerate leftovers.

Makes 4 servings.

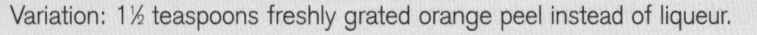

ORANGE-FLAVORED CHERRY SOUP

Variation: 1½ teaspoons freshly grated orange peel instead of liqueur.

4 cups pitted sweet cherries

3½ cups white grape juice
2 teaspoons freshly grated lemon peel
2 teaspoons fresh lemon juice
3 tablespoons orange flavored liqueur

Divide cherries among 4 soup bowls.

Bring grape juice and lemon peel to a boil in a 2-quart saucepan over high heat. Remove from heat; add lemon juice and liqueur. Pour hot mixture over cherries. Garnish with fresh mint sprigs.

Makes 4 servings.

Sides
Stuffing

APRICOT-FIG-CHERRY COMPOTE

Serve with ham or turkey. Or serve with freshly bake gingerbread, or over a dish of vanilla ice cream, for a delicious dessert.

2½ cups water
1 cup granulated sugar
2 cinnamon sticks, broken in half

1 8-ounce package dried Calimyrna figs, stemmed, cut
   and halved lengthwise
1 6-ounce package dried apricots
1 cup pitted dried tart cherries
¾ cup brandy
3 tablespoons chopped crystallized ginger

Stir water, sugar and cinnamon stick in a large saucepan over medium heat until sugar is dissolved. Bring to a boil. Reduce heat to medium-low; cover and simmer 5 minutes.

Add figs; simmer uncovered 3 minutes. Remove from heat. Stir in apricots, cherries and brandy. Return to heat; simmer uncovered until all fruits are tender but still hold their shape, about 10 minutes. Remove from heat; stir in ginger. Cool. Cover; store in refrigerator.

Makes 8 servings.

CARROTS WITH TART CHERRIES

Cherries adds a special touch to this side dish.

1 pound carrots, peeled and sliced

½ cup pitted dried tart cherries
3 tablespoons maple syrup
2 tablespoons margarine
¼ teaspoon ground nutmeg
¼ teaspoon ground ginger

Cover and cook carrots in water in 2-quart saucepan until tender, about 8 minutes. Drain well.

Add remaining ingredients. Cook over medium heat, stirring occasionally, until mixture is hot and bubbly. Serve hot. Refrigerate leftovers.

Makes 6 servings.

CHERRY RICE PILAF

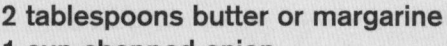

Variation: 1 teaspoon dried herbs instead of fresh.

2 tablespoons butter or margarine
1 cup chopped onion
1 cup chopped celery
½ cup pitted dried tart cherries
½ cup chopped walnuts
1 tablespoon chopped fresh thyme
1 tablespoon chopped fresh marjoram
½ teaspoon ground black pepper

3 cups cooked rice

Heat butter in a large nonstick saucepan. Cook onion, celery, cherries, walnuts, thyme, marjoram and black pepper over medium heat until vegetables are tender, about 10 minutes.

Stir in rice; mix well and cook until heated through. Serve hot.

Makes 8 servings.

CHERRY-SWEET POTATO BAKE

A good side for turkey.

1 40-ounce can cut sweet potatoes, drained

½ cup brown sugar, packed
2 teaspoons cornstarch
¾ teaspoon finely grated fresh orange zest
¼ teaspoon salt
¼ teaspoon ground cinnamon
⅛ teaspoon ground ginger
½ cup apricot nectar or fresh orange juice

1 16-ounce can pitted dark sweet cherries, drained
1 tablespoon butter

Preheat oven to 375°.
Grease an 11x7-inch baking pan. Arrange sweet potatoes in pan.

Mix sugar, cornstarch, orange zest, salt, cinnamon and ginger in a small saucepan. Stir in apricot nectar until smooth. Bring to a simmer. Continue to simmer, stirring constantly, for 2 minutes. Remove from heat; stir in cherries and butter. Pour over sweet potatoes. Bake uncovered 30 minutes. Serve warm. Refrigerate leftovers.

Makes 6 servings.

CRANBERRY-CHERRY COMPOTE

Serve with turkey or pork roast.

½ pound small shallots or pear onions
1 tablespoon butter
¾ cup granulated sugar
½ cup white wine vinegar, divided
1 cup dry white wine
½ teaspoon salt

1 cup pitted dried tart cherries
2 cups fresh or frozen cranberries, do not thaw if frozen
½ cup water

Blanch shallots in a 3-quart saucepan of boiling water 1 minute; drain, peel and separate into cloves if necessary. Cook shallots in butter in a 3-quart saucepan over medium heat, stirring 1 minute. Add sugar and 1 tablespoon vinegar; cook and stir until sugar mixture is golden, about 15 minutes. Add remaining vinegar, wine, and salt; stir 1 minute.

Add cherries; simmer uncovered, stirring occasionally, until shallots are tender and liquid is syrupy, about 45 minutes. Add cranberries and water; boil over medium heat uncovered, stirring occasionally until cranberries burst, about 10 minutes. Pour compote into a bowl; cool completely. Refrigerate.

Makes 6 servings.

SQUASH BAKE

Acorn squash...a favorite in our family.

2 fresh acorn squash

¼ cup butter or margarine, melted
½ cup pitted dried tart cherries
¼ cup chopped pecans
3 tablespoons brown sugar, packed
½ teaspoon ground cinnamon

Preheat oven to 350°.

Cut squash in half. Remove seeds and fiber; discard. Place squash cut-side down in a baking pan (add a little water in bottom of pan). Bake 45–50 minutes or until tender when pierced with a fork.

Stir remaining ingredients in a small saucepan over medium heat until butter melts. Fill squash with equal portions of mixture; stir in gently. Serve immediately. Refrigerate leftovers.

Makes 4 servings.

MUSHROOM FRESH HERBS CHERRY STUFFING

Fresh herbs are used in this bread stuffing.

½ pound bulk pork sausage

2 tablespoons corn oil, divided
1 pound white mushrooms, cut up

1½ cups chopped onion
½ cup chopped celery
2 teaspoons freshly chopped garlic
¼ cup chopped fresh flat leaf parsley
2 tablespoons fresh sage or ½ teaspoon dried sage
½ cup pitted dried tart cherries
1 14-ounce package herb seasoned bread stuffing mix
1 14-ounce can chicken broth
¼ cup butter or margarine, cut up

Stir and cook sausage in a large nonstick skillet over medium-high heat until done. Drain; set sausage aside; discard drippings.

Add 1 tablespoon oil to same skillet. Cook mushrooms over medium heat until lightly browned; place in a large bowl. Add remaining oil to skillet; add onion, celery and garlic. Cook and stir 5 minutes. Add parsley, sage and cherries; cook 2 minutes. Add to bowl with mushrooms. Stir in sausage, stuffing mix, broth and butter. Mix well.

Preheat oven to 350°.
Spoon stuffing into a greased 13x9-inch baking dish. Cover with cooking foil. Bake 50 minutes. Remove foil; bake until top is golden, about 10 minutes. Refrigerate leftovers.

226

Makes 8 servings.

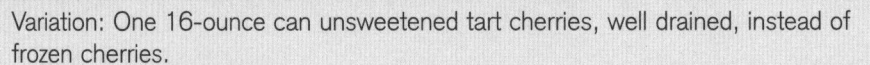

TART & TASTY STUFFING

Variation: One 16-ounce can unsweetened tart cherries, well drained, instead of frozen cherries.

2 tablespoons butter
¾ cup chopped celery
½ cup chopped onion
1 teaspoon dried thyme
¼ teaspoon poultry seasoning

1 7-ounce package dried herb seasoned stuffing cubes
¾ cup chicken broth
2 cups frozen pitted unsweetened tart cherries, thawed, drained

Preheat oven to 350°.
Grease a 2-quart baking dish

Melt butter in a medium saucepan over medium heat. Add celery and onion; cook and stir until tender, about 3 minutes. Stir in thyme and poultry seasoning. Spoon mixture into a large bowl.

Add stuffing cubes and broth; mix. Stir in cherries. Spoon into a prepared baking dish. Cover and bake until very hot, about 30 minutes. May also be used to stuff a 12-pound turkey. Refrigerate leftovers.

Makes 6 servings.

Tortes

DOOR COUNTY CHERRY TORTE

Door County offers another tasty recipe.

Crust
2 cups graham cracker crumbs
½ cup butter, melted
⅓ cup granulated sugar
¼ teaspoon ground cinnamon

Filling
½ cup granulated sugar
¼ cup cornstarch
¼ teaspoon salt
2¼ cups whole milk
2 egg yolks, lightly beaten
1 teaspoon pure vanilla extract

1 8-ounce package cream
  cheese, softened
1 cup whipping cream
1 21-ounce can cherry pie filling

Preheat oven to 350°.

Crust: Mix all crust ingredients in a bowl. Press mixture evenly into an 11x7x2-inch baking dish. Bake 8 minutes.

Filling: Mix sugar, cornstarch and salt in a medium saucepan. Stir in milk and egg yolks; cook and stir over medium heat until bubbly and thickened. Continue cooking 2 minutes. Remove from heat. Stir in vanilla. Cover with food plastic wrap; let stand 20 minutes before spreading over baked crust.

Beat cream cheese and whipping cream in a bowl on high speed until thickened. Spread over custard layer. Spoon cherry pie filling on top. Refrigerate and chill well before serving. Refrigerate leftovers.

Makes 12 servings.

CHERRY MASCARPONE TORTE

Chocolate fudge cake mix is used to prepare this luscious torte.

1 15-ounce can pitted dark sweet cherries in heavy syrup, undrained
½ cup cherry flavored liqueur
1 18.25-ounce package moist dark chocolate fudge cake mix

⅔ cup heavy whipping cream
1 teaspoon butter
1 cup semisweet chocolate chips

1 8-ounce container mascarpone cheese
1 cup heavy whipping cream
½ cup granulated sugar

Mix cherries and liqueur in a small glass bowl; refrigerate 8 hours. Drain cherries well, reserving liquid. Pat cherries dry with paper towels. Prepare and bake cake mix following package directions for two 8-inch pans, except place a circle of parchment paper on bottom of cake pans instead of greasing or flouring pans. When baked, place cake in pans in freezer to chill well. Invert cakes onto a cutting board. Slice each layer in half horizontally to make four layers.

Bring ⅔ cup heavy whipping cream and butter to a boil. Remove from heat; pour over chocolate chips in a small bowl and stir until smooth.

Beat mascarpone cheese, 1 cup whipping cream. ½ cup sugar and ½ cup reserved cherry liquid in a mixer bowl until stiff peaks form.

Place one cake layer on a serving plate; gently dab two tablespoons of reserved cherry juice on top with a pastry brush. Spread with two tablespoons chocolate mixture. Spread ¼ of mascarpone mixture over chocolate. Top with ⅓ cherries. Place another cake layer over filling; press lightly to level. Repeat layering two more times, ending with cheese mixture. Refrigerate until chocolate is set. Refrigerate leftovers.

Makes 10 servings.

MACADAMIA CHERRY TORTE

Serve this delicious dessert warm or cool topped with whipped cream.

½ cup butter

¾ cup all-purpose flour
½ cup brown sugar, packed
¾ cup (3.5-ounce jar) macadamia nuts
½ teaspoon salt

6 egg whites
½ cup granulated sugar
½ teaspoon pure vanilla extract
¼ cup sliced almonds

powdered sugar
1 21-ounce can cherry pie filling

Preheat oven to 375°.
Butter and flour an 8x8-inch square baking pan.

Melt butter in a small saucepan over medium-low heat. Cook, stirring constantly, until butter foams and is a light golden color, about 6 minutes. Remove from heat; set aside.

Process flour, brown sugar, macadamia nuts and salt in a food processor fitted with a metal blade until nuts are very finely chopped; set aside.

Beat egg whites on high speed until foamy. Gradually beat in granulated sugar until glossy and stiff peaks form. Gently stir nut mixture into egg white. Do not over stir. Gently stir browned butter and vanilla into egg white mixture. Do not over stir. Spread batter into pan. Sprinkle with almonds. Bake 35–40 minutes or until a wooden pick inserted in center comes out clean (cover with aluminum cooking foil last 10 minutes of baking). Run a thin knife along inside pan. Cool 15 minutes, then invert onto a cooling rack. Invert again onto a serving plate so that torte is right side up. Dust with powdered sugar. Top each serving with cherry pie filling. Refrigerate leftovers.

Makes 8 servings.

PRETZEL CHERRY TORTE

Variation: Use thawed frozen nondairy whipped topping instead of dry whipped topping.

3 cups crushed pretzels
1 cup butter, melted
¾ cup granulated sugar

2 envelopes whipped topping
1 8-ounce package cream cheese, softened
1 cup powdered sugar
½ teaspoon pure vanilla extract

2 21-ounce cans cherry pie filling

Mix pretzels, butter and granulated sugar in a bowl. Reserve ¾ cup mixture. Pat remaining mixture into a 13x 9-inch baking pan.

Prepare dry whipped topping using package directions.

Beat cream cheese, powdered sugar and vanilla in a bowl. Fold in whipped topping mixture. Spread half the mixture over pretzel crust. Top with cherry pie filling. Spread with remaining cheese mixture. Sprinkle with remaining crushed pretzel mixture. Cover and refrigerate until chilled before serving. Store in refrigerator.

Makes 12 servings.

Miscellaneous

CHERRY PIE FILLING

Home made pie filling...simple to prepare.

2 cups fresh pitted cherries
½ cup water
½ cup granulated sugar
2 tablespoons cornstarch

Cook cherries in water in a saucepan over medium heat 10 minutes. Mix sugar and cornstarch in a cup; add to cherries. Stir and cook until mixture is thickened. Use or store in refrigerator up to 1 week.

Makes about 2 cups.

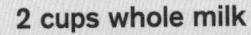

CHOCOLATE CHERRY CUSTARDSICLES

Chocolate cherry custard on a stick...the kids will love these!

2 cups whole milk
5 large egg yolks
¾ cup granulated sugar
2 bars (1.5-ounce each) dark chocolate, finely chopped
2 teaspoons pure vanilla extract
2 cups heavy cream

3 bars (1.5-ounce each) dark chocolate, coarsely chopped
1 (16½-ounce) can Bing cherries in heavy syrup, drained and halved
1 cup almonds, toasted and chopped

Bring milk to a boil in a saucepan over medium heat.
Whisk egg yolks and sugar in a bowl until thick and pale-colored. Add one-third of hot milk to egg mixture, whisking constantly. Pour egg mixture back into saucepan. Continue cooking over medium heat, stirring constantly, until mixture coats the back of a spoon. Do not boil. Remove from heat. Stir in finely chopped chocolate until smooth. Pour mixture into a metal bowl; cool. Stir in vanilla and heavy cream. Freeze 4 hours.

Place coarsely chopped chocolate and cherries on baking sheet in freezer.

When chocolate custard mixture is semi-frozen, process in a food processor until slushy. Stir in frozen chocolate and cherries; stir in almonds. Fill small paper cups to the top. Place in freezer 15 minutes. Insert a clean popsicle stick in each and freeze 3 hours. Freeze leftovers.

Makes 8 servings.

CHOCOLATE COVERED CHERRIES

Chocolate covered cherries...who can resist?

⅓ cup butter, softened
2¼ cups sifted powdered sugar
1–1½ teaspoons whole milk
2 teaspoons cherry liqueur
2 10-ounce jars maraschino cherries with stems, well drained

1 8-ounce package semisweet chocolate squares
1 tablespoon solid shortening

Beat butter in a bowl with an electric mixer on medium speed until creamy. Gradually beat in powdered sugar. Add milk and liqueur; beat until blended. Shape sugar mixture around cherries, coating completely; place on waxed paper.

Microwave chocolate and shortening in a microwave-safe 2-cup glass measuring cup at high 1½ minutes or until melted, stirring twice.

Dip coated cherries by stems into chocolate mixture, allowing excess to drip. Place on waxed paper. Let stand until firm. Refrigerate leftovers.

Makes 3 dozen.

PICKLED CHERRIES

Share a jar.

10 cups sweet black cherries with stems and pits

2 cups water
1 cup cider vinegar
½ cup brown sugar, packed
2 tablespoons pickling salt

Wash cherries; set on paper towels to dry.

Mix water, vinegar, sugar and salt in a heavy saucepan. Bring to a boil, stirring until sugar is dissolved. Pack cherries into hot, sterilized jars. Ladle syrup over top, leaving ⅛-inch headspace. Seal immediately. Process 10 minutes in a boiling water bath.

Makes about 10 cups.

SPICED FRESH CHERRIES

Sugar and spice...and cherries of course!

1 quart fresh sour cherries, washed and pitted
1 cup vinegar
4 cups granulated sugar
½ tablespoon ground cloves
½ tablespoon ground cinnamon

Cook cherries, vinegar and sugar in a saucepan over low heat about one hour, stirring often. After 30 minutes cooking time, add cloves and cinnamon; continue cooking. Spoon hot mixture into hot sterilized jars. Seal and process in a boiling water bath 10 minutes.

Makes about 3 pints.

About the Author

Theresa Millang is a popular and versatile cookbook author. She has written successful cookbooks on muffins, brownies, pies, cookies, cheesecake, casseroles and several on Cajun cooking. She has cooked on television, and contributed many recipes to food articles throughout the U.S.A.

Theresa's other cookbooks
I Love Cheesecake
I Love Pies You Don't Bake
The Muffins Are Coming

Theresa's other current cookbooks
The Best of Cajun-Creole Recipes
The Best of Chili Recipes
The Great Minnesota Hot Dish
The Joy of Apples
The Joy of Blueberries
The Joy of Cranberries
The Joy of Rhubarb

Notes